TERRORISM

TERRORISM
UNDERSTANDING
THE GLOBAL THREAT

revised edition
David J. Whittaker

PEARSON

Longman

Harlow, England • London • New York • Boston • San Francisco • Toronto
Sydney • Tokyo • Singapore • Hong Kong • Seoul • Taipei • New Delhi
Cape Town • Madrid • Mexico City • Amsterdam • Munich • Paris • Milan

PEARSON EDUCATION LIMITED

Head Office:
Edinburgh Gate
Harlow CM20 2JE
Tel: +44 (0)1279 623623
Fax: +44 (0)1279 431059
Website: www.pearsoned.co.uk

First published in Great Britain in 2002
Revised edition (paperback) published in 2007

© Pearson Education Limited 2002, 2007

The right of David J. Whittaker to be identified as Author
of this Work has been asserted by him in accordance
with the Copyright, Designs and Patents Act 1988.

ISBN-13: 978-1-4058-4085-9
ISBN-10: 1-4058-4085-4

British Library Cataloguing in Publication Data
A CIP catalogue record for this book can be obtained from the British Library

Library of Congress Cataloging in Publication Data
Whittaker, David J., 1925–
    Terrorism : understanding the global threat / David J. Whittaker. – Rev. ed.
        p. cm.
    Includes index.
    ISBN-13: 978-1-4058-4085-9 (alk. paper)
    ISBN-10: 1-4058-4085-4 (alk. paper)
    1. Terrorism. I. Title.

HV6431.W483 2006
363.325'12–dc22   2006048470

10 9 8 7 6 5 4 3 2 1
10 09 08 07 06

Set in Goudy by 3
Printed and bound in Great Britain by Clays Ltd, Bungay

The Publishers' policy is to use paper manufactured from sustainable forests.

CONTENTS

BOXES

ACKNOWLEDGEMENTS

I am indebted to Christina Wipf Perry and Heather McCallum of Pearson Education, and to their colleagues, to Marianne Whittaker for invaluable advice and much time in reading drafts, and to Jane Thompson for, once more, producing faultless copies of the manuscript.

Any errors or omissions are entirely my responsibility.

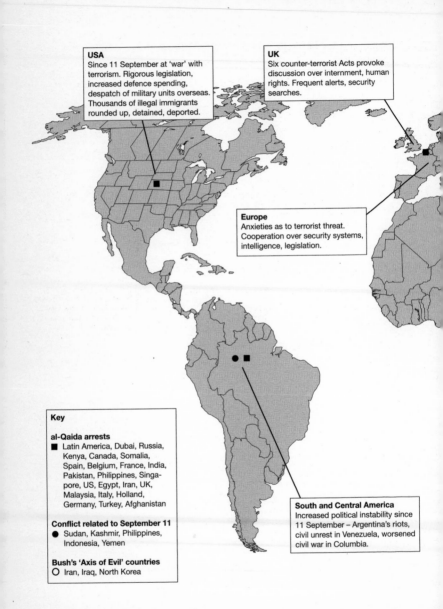

USA
Since 11 September at 'war' with terrorism. Rigorous legislation, increased defence spending, despatch of military units overseas. Thousands of illegal immigrants rounded up, detained, deported.

UK
Six counter-terrorist Acts provoke discussion over internment, human rights. Frequent alerts, security searches.

Europe
Anxieties as to terrorist threat. Cooperation over security systems, intelligence, legislation.

Key

al-Qaida arrests
■ Latin America, Dubai, Russia, Kenya, Canada, Somalia, Spain, Belgium, France, India, Pakistan, Philippines, Singapore, US, Egypt, Iran, UK, Malaysia, Italy, Holland, Germany, Turkey, Afghanistan

Conflict related to September 11
● Sudan, Kashmir, Philippines, Indonesia, Yemen

Bush's 'Axis of Evil' countries
○ Iran, Iraq, North Korea

South and Central America
Increased political instability since 11 September – Argentina's riots, civil unrest in Venezuela, worsened civil war in Columbia.

Israel/Palestinian territories
Sporadic Arab terrorist attacks
bring Israeli counter-measures.
Occasional ceasefires, tentative
negotiations.

Arab world
All Arab states formally
condemned the 11 September
attacks though most criticised the
ensuing Afghanistan war.

Russia
Fundamental shifts in foreign
policies move Russia closer to the
USA with far-reaching implications
for the West.

China
US-China relations much improved
now that Washington has a new
enemy.

North Korea
Included in Bush's 'axis of evil'
despite their condemning
terrorism. Accused of preparing
mass-destruction weapons.
North-south peace process now
set back.

Afghanistan
US, UK, NATO troops struggle to
oust Taliban, restore peace.

South-East Asia
Several governments using war on
terror as excuse to crack down on
internal dissenters e.g. US 'hit
squads' active against Philippine
rebels.

India/Pakistan
India moves against own 'terrorists' in Kashmir, introduces
draconian anti-terrorist laws.
Pakistan rewarded with US aid for
endorsing US Afghan bombing.
India demands end to covert
support of Islamic militants.

Iraq/Iran
Iraq, post-war now occupied by US
and allies. Iran, at first opposed bin
Laden and Taliban but nuclear
ambitions strengthen their hardliners
and risk US confrontation.

INTRODUCTION

This is a new and up-to-date survey of terrorism written with a plain purpose – to inform its readers and to help them understand the nature of terrorism. It has been written with the events of Tuesday 11 September 2001, and of London on 7 July 2005, very much in mind. That day in September was a graphic event for thousands of people around the world. Previously, many of them had shown little direct concern about incidents attributed to violent political action that had occurred in distant places such as Sri Lanka and Israel. Generally, these outrages were deplored if not always discussed and understood. The horrific toppling of New York's World Trade Center and the killing of more than 2,900 office workers brought into universal focus the real possibilities of another heartland being menaced by unpredictable and catastrophic violence. More directly, the carnage illustrated on television screens thrust at viewers a number of disquieting questions. Who could have been responsible for inhuman violence on this scale? Could something like this recur? Where might the next bombing take place? And might we be the next victims?

WHO COULD HAVE BEEN RESPONSIBLE FOR INHUMAN VIOLENCE ON THIS SCALE?

Feelings of outrage and the urge to retaliate are an understandable response to tragic, indiscriminate killings. President George Bush, facing national feelings of revulsion, hastened to call for an international coalition to deal with terrorism as it was said to operate globally. Political leaders in many countries telephoned Washington, readily expressing support for decisive action to counter a threat that might break out anywhere. Their endorsement of US action was not unanimous, however, when it appeared that military strikes against terrorism bases in Afghanistan were being contemplated.

The rhetoric from Washington to 'take out' global terrorism is a predictable consequence of grief, anger and feelings of futility. It does not, however, make it easy to look dispassionately at what took place in New York and at what might happen elsewhere. The word WAR, for a time in the autumn of 2001, was starkly prominent in headlines and media comment. US forces harried Afghanistan, the supposed home of the terrorist leader, Osama bin Laden, with intensive aerial bombing and guerrilla sorties. Yet, war, in a generalized sense, does not seem a realistic way of pinpointing and containing dispersed flashpoints, particularly in terrain like the Hindu Kush mountain range.

Terrorism is more usefully regarded as a most serious breach of peace in which non-state entities participate. They do so in widely separated locations. Thus, it is probably impossible to discern any overall scenario. The picture becomes cloudy and confused.

Terrorists operate in many differing places. They feel impelled to act for a variety of reasons. Few of them call themselves terrorists: many are 'freedom fighters' or heroic defenders of a worthwhile cause. They are frequently admired trailblazers. Some of them, in Cuba, Kenya, Cyprus, Israel, have made a transition from hunted insurgent to state president or

FEW TERRORISTS CALL THEMSELVES TERRORISTS: MANY ARE 'FREEDOM FIGHTERS' OR HEROIC DEFENDERS OF A WORTHWHILE CAUSE.

premier. Today, there are perhaps even 100 terrorist groups whose organizations range from simple to complex and long-lasting. Then, there are a number of states accused as pariahs because they are sponsoring or harbouring suspected terrorists.

A belief much debated after 11 September was that thereafter the world would never be the same again. There were those who saw a second cold war developing, one that pitched into conflict a richly endowed West against a Muslim East where millions languished in poverty under autocracy and religious intolerance. Envy and a fierce hatred of the United States for its closeted wealth and geopolitical intrigues had brought about the September atrocity and might even induce others to do likewise. In many quarters, the counter-response of attack and occupation in Iraq and Afghanistan was felt to be fanning flames throughout Islam. Was the terrorism of 2001 bringing about irreversible change? The best way of beating the terrorists was to continue to live normally. This was the injunction of people as diverse as President George Bush and the novelist, Salman Rushdie. Would it be easy, though, to reconcile irreversible change and calm normality?

We are soon back where we started, peering at a complex pattern of hostile intent, threat and action, without an umbrella label and lacking a magic formula to reduce the global incidence of terrorism.

This book sets out to provide, by way of information, an easy-to-read and concise account of terrorism and, in particular, a scrutiny of how it has shaped over the past half century or so.

WHY DO TERRORISTS HAVE SUCH AN URGE TO RESORT TO VIOLENCE AND WHAT ARE THE COMMON METHODS THEY EMPLOY?

The account of terrorism around the world in Chapter 3 has had to be selective in dealing only with the most prominent terrorist groups. The questions addressed will be considered objectively. Is there a good way to define terrorism? Where does it occur mostly? Why do terrorists, groups and individuals, have such an urge to resort to violence and what are the common methods they employ? Is religious fundamentalism significant? Why do fanaticism and nihilism appear so extreme and inexcusable? Who provides finance to encourage terrorists in their action? Then, there is disturbing conjecture as to the sort of terrorist weaponry that may be deployed in future.

The last two chapters in this book consider how to counter terrorism. Nations, affected by terrorism, have long tried to cope with it as best they could and in a piecemeal fashion. The need now is for international, decisive action to deal with terrorism and so the book ends with a brief account of the counter-terrorism schemes that are being planned.

Finally, there is a section termed 'Where to Find Out More'. This lists a number of easily obtainable sources of further information.

chapter one

THE MEANING
OF TERRORISM

In the autumn of 2001 the word 'terrorism' was on all lips. It was a term prominent in the press and on television. Everybody used it and nobody explained it. The terrible events in New York and Washington on 11 September were constantly recounted in an atmosphere of incredulity and horror. It was not long before all the resources of detection mounted by Washington's administration shone a spotlight upon a distant and impoverished Afghanistan, now pointed out as the refuge of a terrorist group, the al-Qaida. An attack of a warlike nature would be mounted against those held responsible for such a tremendous outrage at America's heart.

Disclaiming any move for retribution, President George Bush urged all nations to work together to rid the world of something that looked like a disease of pandemic proportions. This appeal in a time of trauma was understandable yet it failed to provide a meaning for the term 'terrorism' that the common man could acknowledge. Even more than politicians, media commentators have been slow to give the term full attention. They have neglected an opportunity to throw light on an aspect of human behaviour that is complex and diverse, something that is so specific in its extent and in its context that it cannot be described as a global phenomenon. In the most straightforward of words, what does the term 'terrorism' really mean?

MEANING AND CONTRASTS IN PERCEPTION

Almost certainly, terrorism has a different meaning for those in authority who are responsible for peace, order and security, for those onlookers who are television viewers, radio listeners and readers, for those who are victims or their relatives, and for the terrorists themselves. There are clear contrasts in perception.

In the eyes of a responsible authority, nationally or locally, a workable definition of what they must cope with might run like this: 'terrorism is the premeditated threat or use of violence by subnational groups or clandestine individuals intended to intimidate and coerce governments, to promote political, religious or ideological outcomes, and to inculcate fear among the public at large'. Thus, terrorism is unlawful action, going beyond what are regarded as the bounds of legitimate protest, going further than confrontation, on to exceeding the limits of conventional social behaviour. Terrorism is rated as a criminal offence, wholly disproportionate to any expression of grievance or any attempt to work for change. No civilized community can tolerate licence to kill and the spreading of uncertainty and fear. Strong and stern counter-terrorism is needed

NO CIVILIZED COMMUNITY CAN TOLERATE LICENCE TO KILL AND THE SPREADING OF UNCERTAINTY AND FEAR.

to cope with the targeting of prominent individuals who are murdered or taken hostage. The state will marshal its police and its army and stamp on a threat to peace and a threat to power. Strong-arm tactics of this nature employed in Argentina, Indonesia and Israel are then seen by liberals everywhere as an unacceptable means of dealing with popular protest, however inflamed and violent some of that becomes. In this context, however, it is worth remarking that the relationship between state power and terrorist power can work another way when it may suit the interests of a state such as Libya, Syria or Iraq to give sanctuary to those who would carry out terrorist initiatives beyond its borders. This is state-sponsored terrorism and in many respects it gives terrorism a new meaning.

If terrorism, in the eyes of institutional authority, poses a threat to order, power and peace, then for the onlooker it is a threat to daily life. It is less political and much more direct in its possibilities and consequences. Definition may depend upon circumstances and attitudes and these alter with time. Terrorism as a label may be used to deplore anti-social behaviour which is considered vicious and lethal, for instance, the hijacking of an aircraft, the detonation of explosives, the harassing and shooting of a crowd. There is a ready convergence of condemnation whenever, all too frequently, the press has presented yet another bloody terrorist incident glimpsed in Northern Ireland or in Israel. Sympathy is immediately widespread together with a call for remedial counter-action. For many observers the term 'terrorism' has a wider meaning. The evidence for this is in conversation and in correspondence with newspapers. From time to time, activities branded as malevolent are castigated as 'terrorism'. These may be as various as the burning down of a school, the sabotaging of a farmer's GM crops, the urban rampage of 'football hooligans', or simply bricks heaved through the windows of a corporation identified with that popular enemy, Globalization. This vagueness in definition almost certainly encourages prejudice and intolerance. All too often a leader of protest

THIS VAGUENESS IN DEFINITION ALMOST CERTAINLY ENCOURAGES PREJUDICE AND INTOLERANCE. ALL TOO OFTEN A LEADER OF PROTEST IS DEMONIZED

is demonized and examples of this have been Jomo Kenyatta in Kenya, Archbishop Makarios in Cyprus, Yassir Arafat of the PLO, Fidel Castro in Cuba, and Osama bin Laden in Afghanistan. This then puts them in a state of iniquity until, later, compromise is reached, their status is reassessed, and some of them may even be promoted to head of state.

For the victim, innocent or picked out on account of their status or position, the definition of terrorism bears a grotesque finality. It leads to denial of life, of liberty, of privacy, of human rights. Far more than for any onlooker or security authority, it represents such a degree of transgression that any who survive must feel a sense of irreversible vulnerability. American commentators in 2001, following the horrific bombing of New York and Washington, have speculated that the notion of personal attack spreads far across fifty states, and beyond the bereaved relatives of the lost. In that sense, all contemporary United States citizens are victims.

For the terrorist, the word 'terrorism' may be a misnomer. The actions of those dedicated to a cause may be seen by others as destructive and perverse but for those who believe in what they are trying to achieve the end justifies the means. Here, once more, we meet with a generalization that fogs a clear meaning. The sheer variety of terrorist campaigning down the centuries throws light sometimes on idealists desperate to overthrow a tyrant or struggling to bring about at least some degree of respect and tolerance, a better deal, for the dispossessed and disenfranchised. Exasperation leads to turbulence and violence. Elsewhere, the idealist is balked at every turn and resorts eventually to destructive and inhumane action. Most terrorists claim to be delivering a political message. All too often their methods go further than the question and answer of political dia-

MOST TERRORISTS CLAIM TO BE DELIVERING A POLITICAL MESSAGE.

logue and they come to depend, however reluctantly, upon thrusting only an answer at opponents. For most political activists, among Palestinians, in Latin America, and in apartheid South Africa, there has always been the vision of a more secure and beneficial future. Such is the consuming faith of liberators who are fighting for freedom from dictators, or imperial rule. In other cases, it is the past which transmits a myth, of invincibility, or of their right to live as they prefer. Northern Ireland's paramilitarists appear prisoners of myths and of memories of battles lost and won. Terrorism is not a term that terrorists own to; for the main part their intentions and actions define a duty they feel they must discharge. Generally, they are anxious to claim responsibility for what they do.

HISTORICAL SHIFTS IN MEANING

The term 'terrorism' has shifted in meaning through the centuries. Words still used today by way of condemnation – zealot, thug, assassin – illustrate the changing stress terrorists have placed upon their objectives. In the first century AD the Roman province of Judaea was plagued by the hit-and-run terrorism of the Zealots. There were nationalistic and religious elements in their activities, as there are in numerous terrorist initiatives today. They were zealous in their harrying of Roman officialdom and of Jews whose orthodoxy was tainted with heresy. What in modern language is described as 'religious fundamentalism' played a part in the 1,200 years of terror that the Thugs brought to central and northern India. The 'thuggery' of roving bands was partly religious in carrying out thousands of sacrificial strangulations to the goddess Kali and also criminal in its basis of outright banditry. A faint parallel to modern intolerance among some Muslims was the cult of the Shi'ite Order of the Assassins whose followers considered it a sacred duty to hunt down Christians in Persia, Syria and Palestine at the time of the eleventh- and twelfth-century crusades. Success in their murderous missions would ensure them a place in Paradise, an uncanny resemblance to the reward imagined by modern suicide bombers among the Hizbullah in the Lebanon and the Tamil Tigers of Sri Lanka. It could be said that this was the universal and time-less consequence of violence breeding violence as the defences of Islam were being violated by the cruelties of the Christian West. Indeed, the word 'terror' (derived from Latin and meaning 'a great fear') was taken further by leaders of the French Revolution in 1793–94. They believed that a carefully organized 'reign of terror' ('*la régime de la terreur*') would enable a fragile revolutionary council to order its new-found unity by terrorizing opponents. Robespierre, the high priest of the 1789 Revolution, declared that a democratic France would be a terrorized France. A state-directed system for containing dissension by the most rigorous of means would ensure that France in future was in the hands of a disciplined people.

Increasingly, within the modern era, terrorism is given a sec-ular meaning. Nineteenth-century Russia, more than most other European states, was a hotbed of political debate and intrigue. Terrorism there was, in most respects, an intellec-tual drive to unseat an inflexible autocracy and to replace it with a democratic society. Serfs would be freed. Vast, unwieldy Russia, rich in resources (and resourcefulness), would be liberated and given back to its deserving people. A challenge to the Tsar and his bureaucrats and court was to be headed by a group calling itself the Narodnaya Volya, the 'People's Will', who would choose time and weaponry for terror tactics, as beneficial instruments of delivery. Bomb and firearm must be used without too much shedding of blood. The secretive zones of officialdom were to be infiltrated by spies. The murder of Tsar Alexander II in 1881 was pro-claimed by his assassins as an example of their belief that such an act was an example of what they called 'propaganda by deed'. Terrorism, enshrined in this way, as it were, recruited earnest disciples in St Petersburg, Paris, London and Berlin. Michael Bakunin (1814–76), exiled from his estates in Tsarist Russia, set up in Paris a revolutionary cell whose members called themselves Anarchists, declaring that the evils of capitalism and political oligarchy must be confronted, if necessary, by force of arms. Bakunin, in

ANARCHISTS DECLARED THAT THE EVILS OF CAPITALISM AND POLITICAL OLIGARCHY MUST BE CONFRONTED, IF NECESSARY, BY FORCE OF ARMS.

the 1860s, wrote to inspire fellow-conspirators with his Principles of Revolution and his Revolutionary Catechism. There a definition of terrorism was made plain: the political activist, so frequently alienated from society, was to remain anonymous, a ruthless destroyer of institutions, structures and, where necessary, of those complacent individuals who gave in to exploitation and dominance. The term 'nihilism' was soon coined by others to describe terroristic methods which appeared to have nothing but destruction and disaster as their objectives. Bakunin went to Paris to join Pierre Proudhon (1809–65), the French writer, who might be described as an early philosophical terrorist. For Proudhon, the ownership of property was regarded as theft from the common people. It murdered individual freedom in his view. Anarchy, total destruction, would rid the world of privilege and power, in the army, in the Church, in royal courts and among businessmen.

TWENTIETH-CENTURY TERRORISM

It was during the 1920s and 1930s that terrorism began to acquire a new and ominous meaning. In the hands of a determined clique of power seekers, terror methods could replace the rulers of a democratically elected state with the representatives of an alternative political or ideological creed. The Treaty of Versailles in 1918, ending the First World War, gave a final blow to the old Habsburg and Ottoman empires and brought into being an array of new democracies in central Europe. A consequence of the newness and uncertainty surrounding the creation and growth of new centres of power was a time of uncertainty when expediency and power-mongering led to public unrest and violence in the streets. Countries as dis-

COUNTRIES SAW TURBULENT CONTESTS BETWEEN ADHERENTS OF THE OLD REGIMES AND THE POPULAR FRONTS THAT CHAMPIONED THE LIBERATION OF THE MASSES.

similar as Poland, Greece, Turkey, Romania, Bulgaria, Czechoslovakia, saw turbulent contests between adherents of the old regimes and the popular fronts that championed the liberation of the masses. Pistols, explosives and incendiarism ousted the ballot box and revolutionary terrorists were borne shoulder high as folk heroes. Terrorism was something fought out between the Black gangs of the political right with their secret police and snatch-squads and the Red units of the political left, manning the barricades and resorting to sabotage. Terrorism was now something that used newspapers, loudspeaker vans and radio to spread fear, certainly, and also to recruit legions of followers in a way that had never been possible before the development of these technologies of terror.

A further, expanded meaning of terrorism came about in the mid-1930s as the hopes of the time of Versailles that Europe would now settle down into peace crumbled into cynicism and futility. Now terrorism meant war. Fascist-led states such as Germany and Italy, seeking resentfully and aggressively for a new order, spilled over into neighbouring parts of Europe like Austria and Czechoslovakia, and into Abyssinia and Libya in Africa. Their consolidation of power and the spreading of it depended upon terrorizing opponents at home with summary arrest and possible execution and, abroad, with inhumane military tactics. Hitler's Nazi warplanes blasted civilians in Spain's Guernica and in Abyssinia the forces sent by Mussolini poured mustard gas onto hapless villagers. Terrorism now included genocidal strikes against Jews and gypsies in Germany and the despatch of these contemptuously treated people (the 'Untermenschen') to those houses of correction the world was to know as concentration camps.

THERE WAS SAVAGE INFIGHTING AS THOSE WHO OPPOSED A DESPOT'S TYRANNY WERE CUT DOWN IN RUTHLESS PURGES.

There was now savage infighting in many parts of the world, from Berlin and Bucharest to Valparaiso and Buenos Aires, as those who opposed a despot's tyranny were cut down in ruthless purges. Stalin in the Soviet Union before 1939 sent many thousands of his political opponents, writers and scientists to work camps in Siberia, earning for himself, elsewhere in Europe, the name of 'Master of Terror'.

Terrorism, during the long years of the Second World War, took on new meanings, largely double-sided ones. Terror methods were employed to grapple with a ruthless enemy. Nazi inhumanity towards the inhabitants of occupied Europe, towards so-called 'open cities', and in the treatment of prisoners of war, has been well documented and the methods employed reached new heights of barbarism in character and extent. Those held responsible for such havoc as this were arraigned at the war trials in post-war Nuremberg. Other Nazis or their criminal allies were systematically hunted by the Simon Wiesenthal organisation in the United States, a group dedicated to the tracking down of those associated with war crimes. Equally well-known are the cold-blooded devices of search-and-destroy that the resistance movements in Europe and South-East Asia were forced to devise and deploy. Although many of their methods were cruel and lethal, this resort to terrorism was judged unavoidable and its instigators after victory earned congratulations and medals. Much more debatable was the terror from the skies brought by the Luftwaffe over Europe, the Allied fire-raiding and carpet bombing of German cities, and the nuclear devastation of Nagasaki and Hiroshima in Japan which in so many respects put those military measures beyond the legality of Geneva Conventions. All-out terrorism bringing civilians into the front line was becoming a component of all-out, indiscriminate warfare. The debate over the legitimacy of what seemed to be terrorism-in-uniform and, again, the plight of civilians became anguished with the revelation that the United States had used defoliants and anti-personnel weapons in Vietnam.

Halfway through the twentieth century there was a new emphasis to the meaning of terrorism as the transmitter of a political message. Imperial rule in Africa and Asia was collapsing under the attack of determined cadres of well-informed and carefully organized anti-colonialists. These were 'freedom fighters' in the eyes of stirring masses shaking off oppression and exploitation. These were 'terrorists' as the colonial establishments in London, Brussels, The Hague and Paris branded them in a desperate effort to man the defences. Inevitably, as imperialism was breached, protest erupted into pitched battles and guerrilla warfare. Everywhere the outposts of empire were besieged – in Egypt, Cyprus, Algeria, Kenya, Indonesia (then known as the East Indies) and Malaya. Unavailingly, the colonial powers in retreat stressed what they regarded as the primitive malevolence and lack of civilization of those moving for liberation and self-determination. Eventually, and after much cruelty and suffering, the states that had clung to their empires compromised and granted their former subjects their independence. The freedom fighters, previously so reviled in the circles of empire, had for some years earned the approval of the United Nations for their efforts to set themselves free. Their terrorist excesses were now largely forgotten.

The last two decades of the twentieth century and the beginning years of a new century reveal more than ever the difficulty of trying to define terrorism. Certainly, having considered some of the changes in substance and meaning that the term terrorism has undergone, it must be conceded that it cannot be defined as a global phenomenon. Terrorists, as movers and shakers, will only be reached, to put it crudely, 'where they are'. To deal with them it is important to consider them specifically, case by case. The contemporary world presents terrorism in astonishing complexity and diversity. Equally perplexing are the perspectives through which contemporary terrorism is addressed. Russia fights hard to contain pressure from nationalistic elements on its southern flank, the 'near abroad'. More then ever the pressure has become terrorist in Russian perception whereas in much of the West there is some sympathy for the liberation movement in Chechnya though not for its alliance with Mafia elements in Moscow. Washington struggled for years arming, training and funding a 'contra-revolution' to oust the Sandinista disciples of Che Guevara, the 'guru' of armed revolution by a resolute people, from Nicaragua and San Salvador. They did so against a loud chorus of liberal disapproval in Europe and the United States itself where the American administration was widely regarded as intervening in Central America and backing covert terrorist methods.

> **TO DEAL WITH TERRORISTS, IT IS IMPORTANT TO CONSIDER THEM SPECIFICALLY, CASE BY CASE.**

Liberation movements are not slow to gain sympathy and support elsewhere, although they are forced to use violence, as with the Palestinians, the *mujahidin* in Afghanistan, the IRA in Northern Ireland, and the people of East Timor. There is generally much more divided opinion as to the degree of any support for separatists whose despair quickly earns them the reputation of pitiless desperados. In Spain, unaccountably, the Basque ETA appears to prefer a continuation of terror to a cease-fire and a measure

THE BASQUE ETA APPEARS TO PREFER A CONTINUATION OF TERROR TO A CEASEFIRE AND A MEASURE OF PARLIAMENTARY REPRESENTATION.

of parliamentary representation. The Tamil Tigers in Sri Lanka claim to be supported by an international web of millions of subscribers to their funds in thirty other countries. Neither group would find friends outside their own loyal ranks. Even more generally, as following chapters will illustrate, there is disbelief and disgust over the extent to which modern terrorism has gone to destabilise settled communities, for example, in Israel, former Yugoslavia, Algeria and Northern Ireland. Terrorism, whatever its nature and its causes, now covers a host of means to terrify and destroy. It is not so much anti-social as anti-life itself, when it uses unprecedented methods which bring about thousands of innocent deaths.

MEANINGS AND THE WAY WE USE THEM

In conclusion, a useful meaning of the term 'terrorism' is that it is usually premeditated and carefully planned in secret whether it is to carry out one or more dramatic incidents or to put in place a long-term programme of destruction. A general intention is to coerce a government into accepting changes that have a political or ideological or even religious signifi-cance and to force the hands of auth-ority. An important objective for those terrorists who carry out such a strategy will be to influence the public not so much through articu-late appeal as through intimidation and fear. These are the general assumptions that have influenced the thinking behind this sample of modern and commonly accepted definitions (in addition to the one quoted at the beginning of this chapter):

A GENERAL INTENTION OF TERRORISM IS TO FORCE THE HANDS OF AUTHORITY.

- The use or threat of violence, for the purpose of advanc-ing a political, religious or ideological course of action which involves serious violence against any person or property (British Government).
- Premeditated, politically motivated violence perpetuated against noncombatant targets by subnational groups of clandestine agents, usually intended to influence an audi-ence (US State Department).
- The calculated use of violence or the threat of violence to inculcate fear, intended to coerce or intimidate gov-ernments or societies as to the pursuit of goals that are generally political, religious or ideological (US Department of Defense).
- The unlawful use of force or violence against persons or property to intimidate or coerce a government, the civil-ian population, or any segment thereof, in furtherance of political or social objectives (FBI).
- [International terrorism is] the threat or use of violence for political purposes when (1) such action is intended to

influence the attitude and behavior of a target group wider than its immediate victim, and (2) its ramifications transcend national boundaries (Peter Sederberg).

- A strategy of violence designed to promote desired outcomes by instilling fear in the public at large (Walter Reich).
- Contributes the illegitimate use of force to achieve a political objective when innocent people are targeted (Walter Laqueur).
- The use or threatened use of force designed to bring about political change (Brian Jenkins).
- The deliberate, systematic murder, maiming and menacing of the innocent to inspire fear in order to gain political ends ... Terrorism ... is intrinsically evil, necessarily evil, and wholly evil (Paul Johnson).
- [Terrorism] is ineluctably about power: the pursuit of power, the acquisition of power, and the use of power to achieve political change (Bruce Hoffman).
- [Terrorism] is a tool to be employed, a means of reaching a goal, for many types of political actors ... terrorism is always a method, but under some circumstances in some groups or movements, it is something else ... the means becomes an end (Michel Wievorka).

In a dozen definitions the common ground is obvious. More 'official' definitions stress an institutional attitude to offences against persons and property. Otherwise, threatened action is thought of as potentially terrorist in intention. The FBI even includes 'social objectives' which might give cause for debate. Sederberg's view is rather wider than the others and Johnson's definition seems judgemental. Altogether, in this sample of what has been reckoned to be over one hundred definitions of terrorism, there is a clear lack of objectivity.

Even a brief historical survey such as this reveals that basic meanings are complicated by widely varying differences in character and motivation, and in the perspectives that represent the viewpoint of those who would define. There is simply no universal definition, only, perhaps, a consideration of it example by example.

Terrorism is described by most people as evil, fiendish, irresponsible, unspeakable. It is a cancer to be excised. Given that meaning, as it comes to us in a state of shock and sadness, we are quickly judgemental. It is never easy to be neutral and clearly analytical about something that taxes the emotions. Yet there is a need for that detachment if terrorism is to be understood. There have to be reasons why impassioned adherents to violence, sometimes judged as criminally insane, resort to cataclysmic incidents or long campaigns of fratricide in places so different as Rwanda, Bosnia, Belfast, Sri Lanka, Colombia and Israel's West Bank and Gaza Strip.

THERE IS A NEED FOR THAT DETACHMENT IF TERRORISM IS TO BE UNDERSTOOD.

If terrorism is to be lived with, it cannot ever be accepted. There must be other ways of dialogue – so goes an often repeated assertion which does not advance counter-terrorism very far. By way of looking at the problems terrorism raises, the next two chapters take an enquiring look at the worldwide spread of contemporary terrorism and some of its forerunners. We shall then go on to consider some of the possible motives that lead terrorists to resort to violent action.

chapter two

NEW YORK AND WASHINGTON, MADRID, LONDON

Dates for most of us are fixtures pointing to the inescapable importance of meetings, assignments, financial obligations and pleasurable occasions. Dates such as 11 September 2001, 11 March 2004, and 7 July 2005, though, have a salience that is steeped in horror, death and indiscriminate injury for people in the United States, Spain and Britain. These were the dates when, out of the blue, terrorists savagely attacked a number of great cities.

This chapter outlines the shape of the three attacks, and goes on to deal with the aftermath of each, mainly thinking of the 'shock and awe' of a traumatized public. Government response highlighting security policies and proposed and enacted legislation will be looked at in Chapters 9 and 10.

'NINE-ELEVEN': NEW YORK AND WASHINGTON

The 11 September incident, in 2001, known the world over as 'nine-eleven', was a harrowing catastrophe. Certainly, it was America's 'Bloodiest Day' and 'the Second Pearl Harbor'. A number of hijackers took control of four US domestic airliners flying on internal routes. They crashed two planes into the World Trade Center in Manhattan, New York, collapsing its spectacular twin towers. Soon afterwards the Pentagon in Virginia was struck by a third commandeered plane. A fourth hijacked aircraft, later suspected of being bound for a high-profile target such as the White House or the Capitol, came down into a field in southern Pennsylvania. In this case, passengers had put up a strong resistance with the rallying cry of 'let's roll', only to be subdued at the point of a gun barrel.

Americans were appalled as the casualty figures became clear. In all, there were 2,986 fatalities, including 19 hijackers. All but 400 were the consequence of the World Trade Center blaze and destruction, where an estimated 200 people jumped off the towers down to nearby streets hundreds of feet below. Others, perched on the Center's roof, waited for helicopters that never came.

Responsibility for the attacks was eventually pinned down to agents of al-Qaida, in the view of Washington's 9/11 Commission. Some of the hijackers whose names were made known were 'college grade' with training in science and flying. Their devilish competence can never be in doubt. Somehow they had managed to board aircraft and enter pilot cockpits without arousing initial concern. Since there were no survivors from the lethal flights it is not at all clear exactly how the takeovers progressed save that a number of fragmented reports from anguished passengers using mobile telephones were received on the ground and construed by the FBI.

Al-Qaida, after all, had claimed responsibility for several attacks on US military and civil targets in Africa and the Middle East. To begin with, Osama bin Laden denied involvement in the 9/11 affair. In November 2000, American forces in Afghanistan had recovered a videotape which appeared to show bin Laden planning the attack in some detail. Four years later, in November 2004, a taped statement from bin Laden admitted al-Qaida's culpability for what had happened. Whatever the extent of all this, it is only fringe suspects who have been convicted in connection with the hijacking. There seems little doubt that the nineteen terrorists were entirely committed to an anti-American mission, whether their own protest related to American 'defilement' of Iraq, Afghanistan or the Palestinian community in Israel. Their mode of operation incorporated terrorist suicide, planning that was meticulous, long-term and carefully coordinated, with the aim of causing maximum American casualties and total disregard of other nationals, including Muslims. Warning was never to be given. As a team they were clearly acting in the spirit of the bin Laden 'fatwa' of February 1998 which enjoined the faithful to carry out 'the killing of Americans and their military and civilian allies [as] a religious duty'. This necessitated the launching of attacks on 'the soldiers of Satan'.

THEIR MODE OF OPERATION INCORPORATED TERRORIST SUICIDE, WITH THE AIM OF CAUSING MAXIMUM AMERICAN CASUALTIES AND TOTAL DISREGARD OF OTHER NATIONALS, INCLUDING MUSLIMS.

Something that puts 9/11 in the most horrific of lights is the grim, triumphant message of Osama bin Laden taping his Vision for the World in an Afghan cave as he outlined his preparation for the attack:

> We calculated in advance the number of casualties from the enemy who would be killed based on the position of the tower. We calculated that the floors that would be hit would be three or four floors. I was the most optimistic of them all . . . due to my experience in this field. I was thinking that the fire from the gas in the plane would melt the iron structure of the building and collapse the area where the plane hit and all the floors above it only. This is all that we had hoped for.

THE AMERICAN EXPERIENCE DEMONSTRATES THAT A TERRORIST MAY MOVE BEYOND ALL CONVENTIONAL LIMITS OF HUMANITY, RESPONSIBILITY AND SANITY.

The American experience demonstrates that a terrorist may move beyond all conventional limits of humanity, responsibility and sanity. Foiling such designs in widely separated places certainly taxes everybody's ingenuity and resolve. Nine-eleven was to bring about profound consequences in the United States and elsewhere, concerns that were political, economic, social, cultural, psychological and military. Ways in which the United States attempts to construct a worldwide coalition against terrorists provide much scope for debate and will be outlined in later chapters. It is important here to bear in mind the far-ranging diversity of 'terrorism' and of 'terrorists' that was pointed out in Chapter 1's discussion of definition.

MADRID, 11 MARCH 2004

Madrid's terrorist outrage, 'Spain's 9/11', was entirely different from the American experience, smaller in scale but quite horrendous to Spaniards.

On a spring morning, as commuters and schoolchildren filled trains moving in and out of three of Madrid's suburban railway stations, four of the trains were ripped apart by bomb blast. In a coordinated programme, ten bombs went off, creating tremendous havoc, killing 191 travellers and injuring at least 1,900 more. This mayhem would have been worse had the trains been coming into the Atocha central station or if they had been disgorging their passenger loads there. As it was, Madrid's medical services became severely strained. Makeshift mortuaries were set up in the city centre.

Security forces immediately sealed off all approaches to Madrid and within the central shopping area virtually nobody was able to move far. Forensic scrutinies lasting many hours revealed that the bombs were relatively small devices, each ten kilos or so in size. Terrorists must have brought them to the scene in rucksacks and as each train pulled alongside the platform to disgorge its load the explosive inside the backpack would be detonated from a safe distance using a mobile phone. It was at the Atocha terminus that close circuit television images showed two men heading for the upper level and looking back at the billowing smoke of the explosion some way beneath them.

An immediate question was this: who could have been responsible for these attacks? Could it have been zealots from the Basque separatist organization, Euzkadi ta Askalasuna (ETA), whose nationalist fervour had frequently been underscored by violence for several decades? It had never been on this scale, though. Normally, ETA hardliners had indulged in political assassination and not in indiscriminate acts of this magnitude. They would be unlikely to wreak destruction in Madrid's working-class districts. (A further account of ETA's forceful campaigning is to be found in Chapter 3.) Islamic nationalists, perhaps? Not necessarily from among Spain's very large Muslim community but probably from further east, towards the turmoil of Iraq? Eventually much diligent surveying of the scene and information from 'informers' pieced together a conspiracy scheme bearing down on a North

African origin. Then, as cardinal evidence, a stolen van was found in a Madrid square. Inside there were packs of detonators, rather home-made ones, and a language tape – in Arabic.

The search was pulling in incriminating evidence. An apartment, raided by police a week after the attack, yielded a video disc, again in Arabic. There seemed to be a connection with al-Qaida, confirmed when a chilly voice proclaimed that the attacks on Madrid were an act of revenge for 'Spain's collaboration with criminals Bush and his allies'. Spain must pull troops out of Iraq and Afghanistan. Otherwise, an inferno was promised. Another week brought more confirmation of the conspiracy theories. A London-based Arabic newspaper reported the stern threat of an Islamic brigade established somewhere in Spain. 'Praise be to God', it declared, 'to those who granted us the victory of Madrid and destroyed one of the pillars of the evil Crusader axis . . .' The newspaper went on to give the news of a truce being granted by the brigade to 'the puppets of the United States' until such time as it became clear that Spain's government would respond positively to an Islamic request to pull out of Iraq and not to interfere in Muslim affairs.

The controversy over the originators of the Madrid attack raged over many months, in Parliament, in the media and on every street corner. Some calm ensued when Spain's leading Muslims came together to issue a 'fatwa' declaring specifically that Osama bin Laden had forsaken his

MURDER WAS FORBIDDEN BY THE HOLY KORAN AND WAS, GENERALLY, 'OUTSIDE THE PARAMETERS OF ISLAM'.

religion. Murder was forbidden by the holy Koran and was, generally, 'outside the parameters of Islam'. Even so, the focus of security operations was a very thorough combing of districts where North Africans were living. The searching was ruthless, with seven terrorist suspects apparently blowing themselves up in one Madrid apartment. Snatch squads took in suspects from Morocco, Tunisia and also Syria. Interpol liaison with Italy, France and Belgium targeted suspects whose prominence was international. One Moroccan, known as the kernel of the 'Moroccan Islamic Combatant Group', was charged as team leader with the deaths of all 191 killed, with membership of an armed group, and with the oversight of a terrorist logistics centre in the Canary Islands. The youngest of those rounded up on charges of possessing explosives and of attempted murder was a youth of sixteen.

Madrid's experience of attack was different from America's 9/11 in that those suspected of involvement did not succumb to suicide but stayed alive. Week after week suspects were harried, to be hauled before magistrates and incarcerated before trial. Conviction had to be secured within two years, meanwhile, passports must be surrendered and there had to be weekly reporting. A hundred or so suspects were kept under guard.

For several weeks, tension in Madrid and throughout the Iberian Peninsula was taut. A regime of 'high alert' saw sniffer dogs on the boulevards and armed vehicles cruising the squares. Black mourning ribbons festooned public buildings. In Seville, in Barcelona, there were sporadic controlled

THE COLLATERAL OF TERRORISM, THAT CONSTANT RAW, NUMBING FEELING OF FEAR AND ANTICIPATED SURPRISE HELD MOST SPANIARDS IN SUSPENSE. explosions of suspicious packages and evacuation of whole districts. The collateral of terrorism, that constant raw, numbing feeling of fear and anticipated surprise with an element of stalwart determination held most Spaniards in suspense. It did not, however, prevent 23 million Spaniards from holidaying at Easter for, after all, as their radio told them, 'you can't lock yourself up for ever'. Whether in Madrid, or in New York, day-to-day life will never be quite the same again. Whatever the degree of security provision a people, once blooded, sense the possibility of unpredictable, random violence.

LONDON, 7 JULY 2005

In common with 9/11 and the bombing of Madrid, this was coordinated terrorism. London's transport system was hit as the morning rush hour drew to a close. Three bombs went off in underground trains just outside Liverpool Street and Edgware Road stations and on a packed train moving between Kings Cross and Russell Square. An hour later, a bomb tore off the upper deck of a London Transport bus in Tavistock Square, killing thirteen of the passengers.

The bombings led to severe day-long disruption of transport and movement in the capital. Passengers had first been told that a 'power surge' was closing down the underground system: only gradually did it become clear that the chaos was due to a criminal act of vast extent. Rescue and medical services worked unceasingly and heroically, bandaging bleeding,

blackened passengers and
retrieving the dead. The first
casualty reports gave 53 people
as being killed and more than
700 injured of which half were
admitted to a hospital bed.

**A FACT CAUSING MUCH PAIN AND
CONFUSION WAS THE IMPOSSIBILITY
OF ESTABLISHING WHO MIGHT BE
MISSING AND WHO MIGHT HAVE
ESCAPED.**

Somehow 200,000 people were evacuated from the underground system within the first hour to what were hoped to be
safer areas. A fact causing much pain and confusion was the
impossibility of establishing who might be missing and who
might have escaped. Mobile phones were out of action and
grievous confusion was a result.

Inevitably, the question on all lips was: who could have
done this thing? It did not take too long for police and
security services to work out the logistics. This was partly
because close circuit cameras at Kings Cross station at the
peak hour of 8.30 a.m. had afforded close scrutiny of people's
movements just before the blasts. Particularly useful was the
discovery of personal clothing and documents left near the
bomb scenes which identified the bombers, all of whom
resorted to suicide. This was surely an astounding piece of
luck for those searching for evidence. Piece by piece the
jigsaw could be assembled. Three young men had left Leeds,
travelled by train to Luton and there hired a car which was
later found abandoned. Driving into London they met a
fourth man at Kings Cross station, loaded rucksacks from the
car with high-grade explosives and moved out in different
directions to the sites of destruction. Who were the
bombers? Like the 9/11 attack, the bombers themselves did
not survive. Much, however, became known about them and

their movements as 200 police scanned several thousand phototapes.

They were neatly dressed men in their twenties, unexceptionable in a crowd. Two from Beeston, Leeds, were university graduates, one of them teaching in a Leeds primary school. These were from close-knit Pakistani shopkeeper families who all attended the local mosque. Of Shehzad Tanweer, his mother said: 'He was proud to be British. He had everything to live for ... It wasn't him ... It must have been forces behind him.' (This seems a percipient view in the light of defining terrorism.) As for Hasib Hussain, he was seen as a fanatic – but about cricket when Pakistan played a test match at nearby Headingley. Then there was a Jamaican, Jermaine Lindsay, a 'plodding sort of fellow', looking around at nineteen for a reasonable job. Who had 'infected' them, if that was an appropriate thought? Who was briefing them? Were there 'others', more desperate ones, out there? In what ways might they have 'radicalized' those who became conspirators? Had they learned about bomb making from the internet and then gone as recruits to the 'bomb factory' discovered later in south-west Leeds? As far as could be made out, there was no link with al-Qaida. There is still some speculation as to the motives of others, those who surely indoctrinated the four to be their nefarious agents. Why 7 July? It is true that London had recently been chosen to be the venue for the Olympic Games. At Gleneagles in Scotland, eight world leaders were in consort at an important summit meeting. The connections-

'HE WAS PROUD TO BE BRITISH. HE HAD EVERYTHING TO LIVE FOR ... IT WASN'T HIM ... IT MUST HAVE BEEN FORCES BEHIND HIM.'

in-terror are not obvious except that it might be possible for those so minded to make a chaotic impression upon England, the partner of the aggressive US President. Apart from speculation of this

THE CONNECTIONS-IN-TERROR ARE NOT OBVIOUS EXCEPT THAT IT MIGHT BE POSSIBLE FOR THOSE SO MINDED TO MAKE A CHAOTIC IMPRESSION UPON ENGLAND, THE PARTNER OF THE AGGRESSIVE US PRESIDENT.

sort, there remained the powerful thought that further terror attacks somewhere in Britain could not be ruled out and, if new terrorists were to strike as anonymously as the London four, from an unusual background, what were the chances of preventing another attack?

Something that adds fuel to the last speculation was a failed bombing attempt in London on 21 July, two weeks later. It was another Thursday. Mimicry, possibly, of the earlier 'success'? There were four attempted bombings, with three underground stations and a bus as targets, yet again. It was the detonators going off in plastic food container packages that alerted the police and led, once more, to an organized evacuation of bystanders. There were no injuries. Very likely these bombers were less technically competent individuals. Certainly, a fifth would-be bomber had dumped his device and this proved to be a less than sophisticated model. Again, close circuit photo images of young men with rucksacks helped in the tracing and arrest of four suspects within a week. They were all Middle Eastern in origin and were all convicted of explosives handling.

Unhappily, the next day in July brought grief and much controversy. A Brazilian electrician, Jean Charles de Menezes,

In accordance with Scotland Yard's 'Operation Kratos', and a shoot-to-kill requirement, no police questions were asked.

was fatally shot by a Metropolitan Police squad. His bulky clothing and perhaps his tool bag were thought to betray the would-be bomber. In accordance with Scotland Yard's 'Operation Kratos', and a shoot-to-kill requirement, no police questions were asked. Following what appeared to be a highly unfortunate occurrence, there have been many enquiries, in Parliament and in the media, as to the nature of surveillance, the possibilities of interrogation, the extent of police communication, and the advisability of an 'overkill' strategy. The police, who may yet be blamed for rashness and incoherence, have replied that you cannot take any chances with an apparent terrorist about to act. One supposes that that rejoinder would have been well understood by those responsible for security in New York and Madrid, although there, too, a number of security measures have met criticism where they appear to endanger certain human rights.

You cannot take any chances with an apparent terrorist about to act.

AFTERMATH

THE UNITED STATES

As the smoke clears from a major terrorist incident, it is never easy to discern in the public at large who is overwhelmed by helter-skelter panic and who is grimly prepared somehow to stand upright. There is generally a flood of rhetoric in the press and in the voices of civic and political leaders. Many Americans feel reassured that they can smell conspiracy

AS THE SMOKE CLEARS FROM A MAJOR TERRORIST INCIDENT, IT IS NEVER EASY TO DISCERN IN THE PUBLIC WHO IS OVERWHELMED BY HELTER-SKELTER PANIC AND WHO IS PREPARED TO STAND UPRIGHT.

against the Great Heart of True America. For a good many years they have been used to the fundamental extremism of the disaffected with their war games, posted hate mail and rough riding raids. This time, on the other hand, the enemy is from outside. Certainly in Washington and New York and in the eastern states there was the understandable flush of interest stirred by black-and-white journalism and appeals to patriotism. Steadier thinking was evident as most took to the advice of the State Department in the wake of the attack. Calmness, realism, would win the day. One spokesman said, 'This war [against terrorism] will be fought in shadow and will continue to target the innocent and the defenceless.' The mess-age, no doubt, took some think-ing out among listeners and became clearer when President Bush appealed for resolution and a determined carrying on with business. 'We, all of us', he

'THIS WAR [AGAINST TERRORISM] WILL BE FOUGHT IN SHADOW AND WILL CONTINUE TO TARGET THE INNOCENT AND THE DEFENCELESS.'

pointed out, 'have to cope with a new kind of war, that of killing not only to end lives, but to end our way of life.' Other commentators, less eminent ones, believed that a good way of managing to live with terrorists was to try to understand why they did what they did. There was, too, a wing of critics, some of whom believed that the White House must have had prior knowledge of an attack. A number of them formed a pressure group known as the '9/11 Truth Movement' and busied themselves spreading conspiracy theories, some dubious, others quite fantastic.

Nearer the heart of the debacle and on all sides there was profound gratitude towards rescuers who themselves had suffered grievous casualties. Rudy Giuliani, Mayor of New York, won high praise for his sterling leadership. He was voted Person of the Year by *Time* magazine, leaving President Bush in second place. His administration set about the Herculean task of making New York not only accessible but also liveable. For several weeks, large fires raged. Thousands of tons of toxic debris polluted the air, raising fears of debilitating sickness among relief workers and residents.

Within months of the 9/11 attack there were planners behind the drawing-board. For New Yorkers who felt imprisoned by sorrow and despair, a liberating symbol was to take shape. On the site of the destroyed World Trade Center a new tower block is to arise – the Freedom Tower. One of the world's tallest buildings, the 88 floors will rise 1,776 feet, one foot for every year of US freedom since the Declaration of Independence in 1776. There will be a brass wall plaque on the top floor inscribed America's Freedom – Undefeated.

MADRID

Madrid's horror led to much media debate in the wider world. Readers may be able to follow a particularly interesting and full debate if they visit the internet site *www.opendemoc racy.net*. Styled 'Open Democracy: free thinking for the world', eight writers from six European countries (including

Spain) entered into an on-line debate on 24 March 2004. Their views range over the opinions and fears of Spaniards themselves as well as thoughts from the outside.

ELEVEN MILLION PROTESTERS MARCHED IN SPAIN THE DAY AFTER THE BOMBING, RISKING SAFETY TO MAKE THEIR OUTRAGE FELT.

Spanish popular response is seen as 'courageous'. Eleven million protesters marched in Spain the day after the bombing, risking safety to make their outrage felt. Four days later there was a very solid vote ousting a conservative government and bringing in socialists who would surely be ready to pull the Spanish army group out of Iraq. The point is made that certainly the left in Spain may have seen the new government's willingness to consider disengagement as a positive if terrible consequence of Madrid's ordeal. Had al-Qaida then triumphed? A majority of the debaters believe that both 9/11 and Madrid put up in sharper focus than ever the need to compare what we do about terrorism with what we do, or never do, about the threats to millions of people every year from poverty, famine and environmental degradation, threats prominent in the developed and the developing worlds. If our security position is too narrow, seeing only to the safety of Madrid's streets, then our counter-terrorist strategies are likely to fail. A concluding thought in this debate was that

IF OUR SECURITY POSITION IS TOO NARROW, THEN OUR COUNTER-TERRORIST STRATEGIES ARE LIKELY TO FAIL.

we had an urgent, compelling task: to define and understand different forms of terrorism and their direct and indirect causes. Americans and Europeans now seemed to be facing inevitable riddles all of the time. Who are the terrorists out there? And why do they do what they feel compelled to do?

LONDON

In the past, people living and working in the capital have endured with great fortitude the Blitz years of the Second World War and spasmodic terrorist incidents linked with the IRA. Today's emergency was a sudden, large-scale affair. As daily life returned to some extent of normality, popular response might be seen as shaping in several ways. First, one heard a call for 'togetherness', as it was frequently termed, a call that was expressed spontaneously by community leaders and also a call that was amplified in newspaper articles. Then, on all sides, there was a growing concern to preserve rights and liberties in the face of demands for stringent security controls. Third, a blend of initial sadness and confusion was quite evidently transposed into resolution. Indeed, New York, Washington, London and Madrid appeared to share responses such as these.

A BLEND OF INITIAL SADNESS AND CONFUSION WAS TRANSPOSED INTO RESOLUTION.

Those responsible for public order in government and local authorities were understandably worried about the immediate consequences of the bombing, on the streets. Might a knee-jerk response, a lust for revenge, precipitate race riots? The attack was internal, by four British lads against the British. If some foreign cell were held responsible, reactions might have been less divisive. Would a common view question how far

Islamic people within our own multicultural society were radicalized and so be considered dangerous? Was there not a chance that they would then be ostracized, even met with violence? Fortunately, steadying

WOULD A COMMON VIEW QUESTION HOW FAR ISLAMIC PEOPLE WITHIN OUR OWN MULTICULTURAL SOCIETY WERE RADICALIZED AND SO BE CONSIDERED DANGEROUS?

hands came in powerful messages, from government ministries, London's Mayor, and the Muslim Council of Britain, the latter speaking on behalf of Britain's 1.6 million Muslims. The inevitable association of a war against Iraq and its meaning for Muslims was one thing, London's Mayor, Ken Livingstone, told a vast Trafalgar Square meeting; more importantly, unity and non-discrimination had to be forged. There was an echoing roar of approval from his Muslim and non-Muslim audience when he put it that 'an attack on any of us or by any of us is an attack on us all'. He pointed out that in nearby City Hall a book of condolence had been signed by Sikhs, Hindus, Muslims, Turks and Kurds, all of them genuinely citizens of Britain.

Togetherness was the main theme of a day conference organized by the Metropolitan Police Authority in Westminster, London, a week after the bombing. Invitations were to be sent out to an impressive range of speakers with the aim of sustaining a debate. With the title 'Together against Terror?' the conference would explore the nature of terrorist threats, counter-terrorist strategies, dilemmas involved in protecting our safety and also our rights, and the controversy as to whether the media inform or alarm. Interestingly, the authority invited others, as many as possible throughout the country, to respond to questions in a public poll featured on the police website.

Rights, liberties and freedoms are imperilled if control is rated as pre-eminent. There are those who reckon that 7 July in London was the day when what we set about doing put numerous civilized values in the greatest danger. Standing back in anguish, our over-protectiveness went too far, trampling down some rather frail defences against summary injustice. A number of these arguments and reservations are to do mainly with anti-terrorist legislation hastily proposed and enacted after 7 July and there will be a discussion of this in Chapter 9.

A forthright critic of government response to terrorism in Britain is Baroness Helena Kennedy. Her book *Just Law* appeared shortly before the London attack and she was deeply troubled already by what she discerns as 'contagious abuse' of civil liberties, both individual and collective. She lists certain measures which in today's London aftermath are now even more debatable. These are matters such as the power to intern suspects without trial where the Blair government would have opted for 90 days' possible incarceration, the practice of questioning suspects without adequate legal representation, denial of the right to silence, and the process of accelerated deportation to questionable foreign locales. In our haste to re-order from destruction we must never lower the levels of requiring proof; hearsay is not to be admissible. A second edition of her book would surely stress the dangers and the opportunities that any aftermath puts in front of us.

In the end, aftermath brings resolution and determination clear enough if one peels away the layers of sentiment and high-flown rhetoric that too often obscure realism and practicality. These feelings, of course, are put in different terms. Seven days after the bombers struck in London, The *Guardian* printed an anonymous letter which must have struck common, vibrant chords. Addressed to those who might resort to indiscriminate terrorism, it delivered a sombre message. 'If you are looking to boost morale, our pride, then you have succeeded ... If your aim was to raise our strength and defiance, congratulations ...' And it ended, 'Burning with fear? Not likely! Never!'

chapter three

TERRORISM AROUND THE WORLD

In a small book such as this, it is possible to select and survey briefly only some of the better known of the one hundred or so terrorist groups in the contemporary world. A useful way of doing this is to describe the groups in outline within the continents and countries in which they operate. This chapter considers the incidence of terrorism in the Middle East, Africa, Asia, Europe and the Americas. Some of the motives ascribed to these groups will be discussed in Chapter 4. A number of the methods they employ will be looked at in Chapter 7. The links between terrorism and religion, particularly that known as 'fundamentalism', are dealt with separately in Chapter 5.

THE MIDDLE EAST

Ethnic hostility, the loss of land, and access to fresh water, are elements that have brought turmoil and terror to this region for the best part of half a century. To some extent, rival terrorist groups today represent a spillover from the 1940s when Arab and Jew tried to wrest power and land from the colonial empires of Britain and France. The best-known groups which have used terrorist methods are the Palestine Liberation Organization (PLO) in Israel, and Hizbullah with its base in Lebanon.

The Palestine Liberation Organization was formed in May 1964, first, as a propaganda exercise, and then, with no alternative to violent confrontation in sight, a commando unit, the *fedayeen*, was set up under Yassir Arafat. When each of two disputing parties, in this case the Israelis and the Palestinian Arabs, believe they are in the right, there is no room for compromise. Both rely upon intimidation and terror in a win–win scenario. Palestinian youths since 1987 have pelted Israel's security force with rocks and petrol bombs in the *intifada* (uprising). Israel has retaliated with tear gas, rubber bullets and live ammunition.

EVERY WEEK SEES A CHAIN OF TIT-FOR-TAT KILLINGS AND EXPLOSIONS, WITH THE PALESTINIANS TOPPING THE CASUALTY LISTS.

Every week sees a chain of tit-for-tat killings and explosions, with the Palestinians topping the casualty lists. After thirty years of attrition and deadlocked diplomacy, terrorism does not produce settlement, yet perhaps PLO's very persistence has established them as a legitimate liberation movement. Arafat, once a demon, was, until his death in 2005, received by state leaders anxious to see an end to a volatile Middle East and the establishment of a viable Palestinian state.

Yassir Arafat and a close group of associates managed to bring the PLO out of the darkness into a twilight. Twenty years ago the PLO were condemned as a bunch of fanatical terrorists. Arafat was termed a congenital liar and unscrupulous murderer. The PLO then lost no time in branding Israel as a 'Zionist gangster state'. Complete liberation of Palestine meant the return of Arab refugees and the dismantling of Zionist 'pirate settlements' on Arab land. Arafat, mastermind behind terrorist strategy, was quick to realize that Violence Incorporated met only a stone wall. He was astute enough to change from commander of guerrillas to a 'Mr Palestine', a diplomat who wore a red checked keffiyeh and carried a brief-case rather than a rifle. His moves from Israeli villages to

Lebanon, to Tunisia and back again, dodging Israel's formidable secret police, and his narrow escapes from assassination, earned him the nickname of 'Great Survivor'. That would be an appropriate name for the PLO itself, whose leaders now have

MODERATION RATHER THAN EXPLOSIVE ANGER HAS TAKEN THE PLO FURTHER THAN THEY COULD HAVE IMAGINED.

documents and tape recorders as ammunition in search for compromise, 'interim agreements', and well-rehearsed appeals to Western media and statesmen. Moderation rather than explosive anger has taken them further than they could have imagined – a Nobel Peace Prize for Arafat (and a red carpet for him elsewhere) and the setting up in real business of a Palestinian Authority on Arab land in Israel.

Unfortunately, and despite the moderation and realism among many Palestinians and liberal Jews, there is flaring conflict and a fragile edge to daily existence. Splinter groups on the Arab political Left opt still for political assassination, sniping and car bombing. In Israel itself, Tel Aviv insisted that unless Arafat could pull back the toughest fighters from yet more violence there could be no peace and no restoration of land rights. To the Jewish demand 'no land without peace', the Palestinians reply that there will be no peace without the promise and putting into effect of land redistribution. 'Stop all the terrorism' was the order to Arafat and his clique. If the PLO does nothing there will never be dialogue between Arab and Jew. And terrorism will flourish as each side strives for advantage.

Other Palestinian organizations which may be termed terrorist are the Islamic organizations, Hamas and the

Palestinian Islamic Jihad (PIJ), and the Left-wing organizations, the Democratic Front for the Liberation of Palestine (DFLP), the Palestine Liberation Front (PLF), and the Popular Front for the Liberation of Palestine (PFLP). In Lebanon itself, Hizbullah is a powerful presence but because it is strongly religious as well as political it will be discussed later, in Chapter 5. Members of these groups would call themselves fighters for freedom.

THE LAST THREE TO FOUR YEARS HAVE SEEN A SHIFT OF ISLAMIC TERRORIST INFLUENCE FROM THE MIDDLE EAST TO CENTRAL AND SOUTH ASIA.

Although the Middle East – Israel, Lebanon, Syria – remains the centre for much of the world's terrorist activity, the last three to four years have seen a shift of Islamic terrorist influence from there out to Central and South Asia. Some of the reasons for this relate to the disappearance of the old Soviet Union, its unexpected defeat by the freedom fighter *mujahidin* of Afghanistan, the increased counter-terrorism collaboration among Arab countries, and expanding nationalism in the Balkans. Now, there is more prominence to Muslim feelings of solidarity in the Caucasus and in republics such as Kazakhstan, Uzbekistan and Chechnya (a worry to Moscow), in the Balkan lands of Kosovo and Albania, in Afghanistan, and in the Philippines. Ominously, there are signs in most of these places of internal dispute and conflict which may explode into religiously influenced terrorism.

Nevertheless, back in the Middle East lands, the fiercest terrorist groups have fastened a double-edged grip on Arab people. In the first place, they have managed to foster in

Arab minds the idea of a West–East confrontation where there is a conspiracy against Islam's religion and way of life. This has not been too difficult to do in those countries where large numbers of poor peasants have little religious knowledge and much sense of protest at the hard lives they must lead. The idea of someone having to carry out a crusade, a *jihad*, even one of force, is not really foreign to them. It becomes a duty on all believers to face down an infidel West and, in so doing, all means of counter-activity are justified. The duty to defend 'true Islam' embraces a need to work against the arbitrary oppression and corruption

> **IT BECOMES A DUTY ON ALL BELIEVERS TO FACE DOWN AN INFIDEL WEST AND, IN SO DOING, ALL MEANS OF COUNTER-ACTIVITY ARE JUSTIFIED.**

that the West has propped up in places such as Saudi Arabia and Kuwait. Terror methods may then be the only means of fighting against heresy and injustice, whether this is in Western or Arab guise. Campaigning to consolidate Islam against non-believers has been a task energetically pursued not only by religious leaders but also by a core of middle-class professionals – engineers, physicians, lawyers, academics, businessmen – who have perhaps regretfully acknowledged that in some circumstances a violent struggle may be necessary to put across a message. Added to the groundswell of public sympathy for standing firm against injustice and disbelief, there is also a readiness to meet its financial costs. Both in the Muslim world and among Muslim communities in the West there is massive fundraising by political, social, educational and charitable groups and projects. Institutions and individuals in such countries as Saudi Arabia, Pakistan, Iran, Kuwait, Bahrain, Sudan are able to donate immense sums to what they innocently regard as support of their religion and their culture. Most of them, particularly those living in communities in non-Arab lands, would be horrified if this money were seen to be siphoned off to a front organisation to fund, however indirectly, violent political activity or terrorism. It is more likely (according to US State Department investigators) that certain terrorist networks find ways of hiding behind the legitimate activities of charities and then divert or launder some of the proceeds. Some financial support of terrorism does come from the production and handling of narcotics, above all in Afghanistan and Pakistan; otherwise, there is not a large amount of corruption or crime.

INSTITUTIONS AND INDIVIDUALS ARE ABLE TO DONATE IMMENSE SUMS TO WHAT THEY INNOCENTLY REGARD AS SUPPORT OF THEIR RELIGION AND THEIR CULTURE.

The PLO has gone for respectability, as we have seen. This is less the case with other groups such as Hamas and Hizbullah. In so many respects these remain fanatical organizations and this aspect of them will be looked at more closely in Chapter 6. Hamas, though, has just won governmental representation, as Chapter 6 will also discuss. At this point it is useful to say something about the terrorist transit that goes on between these groups and their nearby backers in Syria. Hamas, long ago, decided to locate its headquarters, training camps and barracks over the border in Syria away from the clutches of Israel's counter-terrorist units. Damascus has a guarantee of sanctuary, a useful airport, and the technical facilities of the media, that the terrorist planning weapons-smuggling, propaganda exercises and the next ploy against Israel could never

secure nearer home. That, too, is where the terrorist com-
manders live and work.

Hamas recruiters continue to visit universities in Syria,
Yemen and Sudan pinpointing a fresh generation of sympathizers. Other agents mix with Arab students in Europe. The
'trade' is highly organized and clearly fills up the ranks of the
dedicated. It is not altogether easy for Syria and Lebanon to
be seen indulging in terrorist sponsorship. Their doubtful
connections are condemned by the West and there is a risk of
diplomatic sanctions and economic boycott. Certainly in the
case of Syria, the rulers and government have wanted to
strengthen a personal and national image of defending the
Arab cause and of not weakly kowtowing to pressures from
the United States and Israel to put an end to terrorism. On
the other hand, Syria and others must now be realizing that
the United States, after the disaster of 11 September, is going
to come down very hard on any terrorist cells and their backers. Will Syria now 'surrender' any form of terrorist support to
growing international demands? Is there a chance that compromise in this direction might make it easier to have meaningful talks with the old enemy, Israel?

AFRICA

Libya and Algeria are places associated with terrorist activity
on a grand scale, the first as exporter of terrorists and the
second as an arena for pitiless fratricide.

Libya is a case all on its own. Libya's leader, Colonel
Muammar al-Quaddafi (also known as Qaddafi or Khadafi)

Box 1

A terrorist incident

Place

Rome/Cairo flight then Beirut, Algiers, Beirut, 14–30 June 1985

Incident

- 3 Hizbullah terrorists hijack TWA 847 en route. Demand release of 776 Shi'ite Palestinians in Israeli prisons.
- Aircraft flown on to Beirut, then Algiers, then back to Beirut.
- At each stop non-US passengers, women, children let off leaving 39 US men aboard.
- Final stop Beirut. Men taken off, hidden around city to make rescue difficult. Held for 17 days.
- USA asks Israel to agree terrorist demands and release at least 756 prisoners. US men freed.

Consequences

- USA and President Reagan appear helpless and 'soft'.
- USA sees intense media coverage as obstructing US attempts to secure hostage release. Also media needlessly magnify incident, manipulate incident unhelpfully.
- Hizbullah morale boosted, jubilant at getting maximum publicity at little cost.
- Israel discomfited by world focus on their 'abduction' and jail policies in 'occupied' Palestine.

has been cast as a demon much more readily than Yassir Arafat. In the eyes of many in the West, the staple export of his Libyan regime is terrorism, although, in fact, Libya as a state has undergone a number of remarkable transformations. A North African backwater, much of it desert peopled by many impoverished tribesmen, Libya became prosperous in the early 1970s with the discovery and exploitation of high-quality oil reserves. A group of young army officers backed by students and journalists and captained by Quaddafi were then able to wrench power from an effete monarchy in September 1969 and with a potent cocktail of nationalism and socialism to set about 'freeing the people' and building a unified state. To begin with, the focus of a new enterprise was the building of a unified state, the Jamahiriyah. Eventually, though, through the medium of a revolutionary catechism and radio broadcasts, Libya went on the defensive towards the enemies it saw around – Communists, infidels in the view of Islamists, foreign commercial interests and capitalists. Inevitably, the United States, as a citadel of capitalism, became a prime target, at first, for invective, and then for more martial hostility. Other countries seeking to throw off imperial or capitalist shackles, such as Angola, apartheid South Africa, the Philippines and Northern Ireland, would be helped in the sacred cause of befriending national liberation fighters.

For many in the rest of the world, Libya, after ten years of independence, was acquiring the reputation of a trouble stirrer. Libya was now deploying infamous terrorists egged on by Quaddafi, a bellicose whirling dervish (in American words, at least) and, worse still, intervention like this went beyond political interference in neighbouring countries to backing

INTERVENTION WENT BEYOND POLITICAL INTERFERENCE IN NEIGHBOURING COUNTRIES TO BACKING RANDOM HORRIFIC ACTS OF TERRORISM ALL ROUND THE WORLD. random horrific acts of terrorism all round the world – in Europe, in Africa and in Asia. Death squads and 'hitmen' roamed far afield to airports in Vienna and Rome, to US barracks in Beirut and Germany, to a Berlin nightclub frequented by American GIs, and to an embassy in a London square where a policewoman was murdered. Foreign aircraft were bombed, a Pan Am flight over Lockerbie in Scotland in December 1985 and a French passenger jet in August 1989. Quaddafi's mercurial adventurism looked ever more irresponsible and irrepressible when he authorized a destructive expedition into the former French colony of Chad and when his Libyan aides were urged to organize coups in Saudi Arabia, in Algeria and in Tunisia. To the horror of the West, Libya held conferences on terror methods, in Baghdad, Tripoli and South Yemen.

Libya's policy of random terrorism was becoming a grave international menace and so anti-American that President Reagan despatched a punitive air strike against Quaddafi's Tripoli headquarters in April 1986. This was perhaps a rather hasty and not very successful move since it consolidated Libya's resolve and recruited many like-minded Arabs. More effective measures of branding Libya as a pariah state were the expulsion of its diplomats from the majority of states and the imposition of economic sanctions, backed by the United Nations.

International condemnation of a state such as Libya and one sanctifying terrorism might have continued for ever had not

Quaddafi, never very consistent as a political strategist, shown signs of relenting over his sponsorship of violence. This might have had something to do with his shrewd calculation in 1991 that his country's oil wells were an attractive proposition to Allied nations ending the Gulf War that year. Terrorists now changed tactics and entered the marketplace.

Almost eight years went by before the penitence of Libya was internationally recognized, sanctions were withdrawn and normal diplomatic relations re-established. Terrorism had come out of the cold. Even more intriguingly, Muammar al-Quaddafi, in September 1999, presided over a summit of twenty African presidents. The arch-terrorist spoke again as a unifier, only now it was as a thoroughly respectable pan-African 'leader of peace and development'.

TERRORISM HAD COME OUT OF THE COLD.

Libya is a leopard which has managed to change its spots. This is not the case with Algeria, torn by bitterness and butchery for nearly fifty years. France, after 1945, had held on to Algeria, as a colony, without paying much attention to the obvious need and clamour for social and economic improvement. Independence was reluctantly granted amid chaos and bloodshed in 1962 and if the new administration had been able to weld together discordant political and religious strains a descent into lawlessness and terror might have been averted. Algeria was to fall apart as political bands took up arms in rivalry. Leading the fray was the Front de Libération Nationale (FLN) assigning its leader, Ahmed Ben Bella, as the first Prime Minister, certainly, but also showing its teeth in declaring that a hundred Frenchmen would pay for the loss of one of its

THE FLN SHOWING ITS TEETH IN DECLARING THAT A HUNDRED FRENCHMEN WOULD PAY FOR THE LOSS OF ONE OF ITS FIGHTERS FOR FREEDOM PARTISANS. fighters for freedom partisans. Then, there were the Groupe Islamique Armé (GIA), the Front Islamique de Salut (FIS), and the Mouvement Islamique Armé (MIA).

It might be thought that the followers of Islam might be able to restrain their more militant comrades. Not at all. Mayhem in town and countryside was the by-product of religious zeal and plenty of ammunition. The partisans gunned down state employees, priests, nuns, journalists, professors, foreign visitors. Algeria became a no man's land, the most dangerous place in the world. Terrorism, it is reckoned, cost the lives of 20,000 people in the years 1992–97. Algeria's government, for three decades, has stayed bewildered and irresolute. Early attempts at reasserting peace sent out an ill-disciplined security force, part French, part native-born, with the inevitable consequence of indiscriminate shooting and pillage. Later attempts at getting rid of terrorism resulted in a fury of arbitrary arrest, **USING TERROR TO EXPEL TERROR ENLISTS A LEGION OF TERRORISTS.** internment camps and frequent execution. When government counter-action lends force to its slogan of 'kill one to scare a thousand', the consequence is predictable: using terror to expel terror enlists a legion of terrorists. Algeria's terror was understood and the FLN was given funds and weapons by Lebanon's Hizbullah, and by Sudan and Egypt.

Algeria today is lacerated by a variety of terrorists who sweep mercilessly at anybody in their way. A UN report in 1998 found a country in complete disarray as random killing and burning affected the whole population. Terrorism was beginning to bring an entire country to its knees. Most unhelpfully, the Algerian government (sometimes turning a blind eye to excess among security personnel) insists still that Algeria alone has to deal with Algerian terrorism. This might be understandable if that government was not so divided and defeatist that it makes a mockery of today's need for international action to deal with the international scourge of terrorism.

Algeria has gone from bad to worse. In other places, not everything has worsened. Libya courts respectability. Syria, formerly ostracized as state sponsor of terrorism, has been courted by others, by the United States and Britain, in a drive to enlist support for an anti-terrorism coalition.

ASIA

If Algeria is rated as the world's most dangerous place, then in second place must be the island of Sri Lanka (formerly the British colony, Ceylon). A furious quarrel has raged there since shortly after the British left in 1948. Two terrorist factions have held the land in their grip, the People's Liberation Front (JVP), named after its founder Janatha Vimukthi Peramuna, and the Tamil Tigers (LTTE), the Liberation Tigers of Tamil Elam. It is mainly the Tigers that have Sri Lanka, and its capital Colombo, in continuous fear despite frenzied attempts by the security forces to drive them out. They are unhesitating in calling for a separate state for the Tamil minority (one in five Sri Lankans) to be known as Eelam. The intensity of the conflict on the island is materially

THE INTENSITY OF THE CONFLICT ON THE ISLAND IS MATERIALLY AIDED BY A GLOBAL NETWORK OF FELLOW TAMILS. aided by a global network of fellow Tamils, reportedly 70 million of them living in such places as Europe, South Africa and North America. They may not subscribe to violence but they do subscribe millions of dollars to Tamil funds, and they provide eager disciples to promulgate a separatist cause using an internet site called Tamilnation, as well as television, videos, radio and newspapers. Those in Sri Lanka and elsewhere who are enthusiastic separatists speak of the 'growing togetherness' of Tamils wedded to the ideal of building a self-determining nation.

As long ago as 500 BC, say the Tamils, they came to Sri Lanka from south-east India. They base their appeal for separateness on length of residence and the distinctiveness of their rich culture which owes much to Hindu beliefs. They complain bitterly that the Sinhalese majority, largely Buddhist, has always been oppressive and intimidating. Their campaign, though, has become a relentless struggle and a bloody war since all the concessions by Colombo governments which were offering some degree of autonomy have been rejected. A fact making agreement difficult is the religious divide between the Sinhalese and the Tamils but more crucial than that is the dogged belief in eventual victory among Tamils who took up Marxism to begin with and then went on to follow the revolutionary ideals of Che Guevara and Fidel Castro. There is terrorism in the crowded towns and guerrilla warfare in the countryside.

Perhaps 6,000 Tiger fighters operate stealthily laying siege to barracks and airstrips and now and then rounding up villagers they accuse of government collaboration. They are well armed with automatic weaponry, high explosive and surface-to-air missiles procured from Burma, Thailand, Lebanon and Quaddafi's Libya. One recent estimate is that they have lost at least 10,000 of their number but these are soon replaced by an 'Unceasing Wave' of teenage terrorists. Their vicious attacks have taken the lives of many thousand army personnel, including 1,200 in the destruction of a barracks. Civilian deaths continue to rise and the latest toll is some 60,000 together with seventeen assassinated politicians.

There are no very dependable signs of any real ending of the terrorism in Sri Lanka, chiefly because the remorseless zeal of Tamil fighters is never lessened by their savage losses; if anything, it is increased in a spirit of martyrdom. Undoubtedly, as with the Hizbullah in Lebanon, there has always been with the Tamils a cult of martyrdom and an expectation that victory may be gained even if it means suicide. We shall have more to say in Chapter 6 about the fanaticism and suicide that characterizes some forms of terrorism. There is every reason to believe that younger, impressionable Tamils are prisoners of the myth of the revolutionary hero, destined to conquer at all costs. A belief such as this must reinforce a feeling of distinctive Tamil identity and lend strength to aggressive intentions. Sri Lanka's terrorism, strengthened by global sympathizers, has an international dimension. Peace negotiations, brokered by Norwegian intermediaries, have taken place spasmodically since February

THE REMORSELESS ZEAL OF TAMIL FIGHTERS IS NEVER LESSENED BY THEIR SAVAGE LOSSES; IF ANYTHING, IT IS INCREASED IN A SPIRIT OF MARTYRDOM.

2002. Eventually, a tentative ceasefire has been arranged. Sri Lanka's coast unfortunately did not escape the tsunami disaster of December 2004 and this undoubtedly has concentrated all minds on the inescapable need for unity. From time to time there are bloody violations of the peace as truce talks in Colombo and Geneva inch forward, the consequence, so it is said, of rogue elements among Tamils who are grimly reluctant to give up a struggle.

There is a world focus on Asian terrorism in the case of Afghanistan and its harbouring of Osama bin Laden's organization, al-Qaida. This is very much a fanatical corps and it will be looked at more closely in Chapter 6. Apart from this, there is a contemporary twist in an account of Asia's terrorists, and that is the spectacle of two nuclear rivals, India and Pakistan, eyeballing each other ferociously at the beginning of 2002 over the borderland of Kashmir.

Kashmir is a dispute nobody has been able to settle since India left the British Empire in 1947 and the country became everybody's irritant. Hindus ruled a mainly Muslim population and they high-handedly took the Kashmiris over to India. The UN suggestion of a referendum was never implemented. India and Pakistan have twice come to blows over Kashmir. The

THE PROSPECT OF A WAR BREAKING OUT BETWEEN TWO NUCLEAR GIANTS IS A FRIGHTENING ONE.

prospect of a war breaking out between two nuclear giants is a frightening one. Within Kashmir and for half a century there has been a relentless struggle for liberation. Tension between Pakistan and India worsened after an attack on New Delhi's parliament building on 13 December 2001 in which fourteen Indians and five gunmen died. India was outraged – they were Pakistani terrorists striking at India's heart. A 'proactive and hot pursuit' policy was the only one possible. Each side deployed thousands of border troops. No talks were likely before Pakistan emptied its lockers of terrorists. Britain's Prime Minister, Tony Blair, went out to do what he could to prevent Asia exploding.

Pakistan's President, General Musharraf, did not help the situation by making a distinction between acts of terrorism which he condemned and what he called 'legitimate resistance and freedom struggles'. Delhi was furious. Was this not a falling back on the old 'freedom fighter' distinction just to put Pakistan's case for Kashmir in a favourable light? It could mean war, using words in that fashion.

To everyone's relief, the soldier Musharraf began to search for a less military way out of the crisis. His police were sent to round up 200 members of 'terrorist' organizations, mostly responsible for sectarian violence. India appeared unimpressed. More than a gesture was wanted. 'The eradication of terrorism', the Indians stormed, 'is not a public relations exercise. These are substantial issues ... and must be addressed seriously.' On all sides, it seemed, there were more hawks than doves. Pakistan generals claimed that the arrests were Pakistan's drive for internal security and could have nothing to do with India. There was talk, too, of radical

ON ALL SIDES, IT SEEMED, THERE WERE MORE HAWKS THAN DOVES.

political elements in Pakistan being keen anyway to let terrorist squads harass Hindus. They insisted that no President should give in to India's brusque demands.

The military stand-off has cooled since 2002. Musharraf's statement that 'Pakistan rejects terrorism in all its forms and manifestations and is fully cooperating with the international coalition against terrorism' has eased things considerably. Meanwhile, Kashmir remains an unsolved problem and the lair of the most resolute terrorists in Asia.

TERRORISM IN EUROPE

Europe, particularly, has seen in the Balkans, in the collapse of Yugoslavia after 1991, an almost incredible viciousness among neighbours who once lived peacefully side by side. In Serbia, Bosnia, Kosovo and Macedonia, murder, rape and pillage have decimated communities and led to the flight of 2 million refugees. There is ample evidence from the witness of UN peacekeepers, in the press, and before the war crimes tribunal in The Hague, of the wide incidence of terror tactics, above all in the horror of 'ethnic cleansing'.

As a new century starts, there are in Europe terrorist scenarios which have at least one thing in common: terrorism is in suspense. In the Basque region of northern Spain and in Northern Ireland, terrorism is entrenched, latent and sometimes vibrant. Despite ingenious and patient negotiation, the tabling and signing of agreements, with ceasefires and concessions, and in the face of much public condemnation, terrorism has not altogether disappeared. Two questions are starkly clear. How is it that terrorists in these places persist with their offensives? Why do they go on believing that violence paves the way forward?

WHY DO THEY GO ON BELIEVING THAT VIOLENCE PAVES THE WAY FORWARD?

SPAIN

First, then, the enigma of ETA in Spain. The Basques are an ancient people with a unique language and proud traditions. Three million of them live in seven provinces along the Franco-Spanish border. Their corner of northern Spain is no longer cut off from mainstream industry and commerce, for with the discovery of high-grade iron ore Basques have left the farmyard for the steel mill and shipyard. This is one of the reasons why a flood of immigrants has now altered Basque ways of life for good. Does the disappearance of an older lifestyle and its replacement with new, challenging expectations lead to discontent and tension and feelings of alienation? Observers have frequently thought this. Or, could it be that being marginalized for centuries by Madrid, added to the realization that Basques deserve a reasonable degree of autonomy, together have pushed patience over the edge? As long ago as 1959 a group of Basque students and journalists founded a party to be called the Euzkadi ta Askatusuma, Basque Homeland and Freedom, the ETA. To begin with, their campaign would focus on independence for the Basques and the revitalization of their language and culture. For some of the members this emphasis lacked a political thrust. The only way forward was to unleash drastic strong-armed measures against which Franco's government would have no chance. Yet in the mid-1960s, rather slowly, it is true, Madrid was restoring civil liberties and even allowing open expression of independence demands. Nevertheless, a phase of discord and disruption was to ensue with no Basque feeling safe to move about or work as normal.

With the death of the dictator, Franco, in 1975, the number and frequency of terrorist attacks against the authorities actually increased sharply. It was as if the momentum of violence was unstoppable. The most effective agent of change was a destructive one. Nothing and nobody need be spared.

WHAT BEGAN AS A MOVEMENT FOR NATIONAL LIBERATION HAS BECOME, IN THE LAST TWENTY YEARS, A LIFE-OR-DEATH STRUGGLE OF SEARING INTENSITY.

What began as a movement for national liberation has become, in the last twenty years, a life-or-death struggle of searing intensity. Basque townspeople have found their daily lives torn by anxiety and uncertainty as to whether their homes and workplaces might be burned down. A car parked next to a neighbouring shopping arcade might go up in flames, spraying shrapnel. The mayor might be shot or kidnapped for a ransom. Violence has also crossed over into France since ETA has seen the security arms of Madrid and Paris colluding to bring them down. Weapons have been imported from such places as Libya, Czechoslovakia and Russia. Active liaison was even established with some units of the IRA. There were few clear lines distinguishing what appears to be nationalistic frenzy and the criminal exploits of extortionists and bank robbers.

The last twenty years have seen attempts to bring the terrorist and the security authorities into contact and negotiation. Madrid and the Basques have put a ceasefire in place on several occasions only to have the arrangement aborted. Very much as in Northern Ireland, a peace agreement has depended upon the Basques laying down arms completely but when this failed to materialize, again as in Belfast, a phased disarmament was thought possible, together with the release of prisoners. It is not easy to see why terrorism continued to break out in a reasonably prosperous community when the insurrection appears to have little point and is roundly condemned by most of the public.

The moment of resolution perhaps arrived in late March 2006. It was then that ETA leaders declared a 'permanent' ceasefire. The aim, so they declared, was 'to promote a democratic process in the Basque country and to build a new framework in which our rights as a people will be recognized'. Never before had a contrived ceasefire been termed 'permanent'. Spain's Socialist government expressed caution and hope that terror methods would be renounced to allow for dependable exploratory talks in Madrid.

NORTHERN IRELAND

Northern Ireland has been a place of turmoil and terror for many years. As with the Basques in Spain, there is a tantalizing question: is it peace or is it not? What can justify a resort to violence when nominally issues have been settled, a peace regime has been agreed, and at least some disarmament has been secured? It is often suggested that Ireland is a land of long memories and cherished myths. Northern Ireland was settled 300 years ago by 'foreigners' from the British mainland and then ruled high-handedly by absentee landlords and an apathetic London government. Understandably, the fact of that, and of an inevitable nationalistic urge for self-determination and self-government, gives some colour still to long striving for social and economic rights and for emancipation. The Catholic minority in Northern Ireland styles itself as Nationalist or Republican and girds itself for a drawn-out struggle against Protestant Unionists. Memory gives point to contest in Belfast and the six counties of Ulster. It is memory which has armed rival brigades – the Irish Republican Army (IRA), since 1919, advancing the Catholic cause alongside the political party of Sinn Fein, and the Ulster Unionists, determined to prevent a united Ireland and their cutting off from London.

It is memory which has soured a contest so much that in 1969 the IRA launched an all-out attack on what it regarded as an oppressive British establishment. No terrorism of this sort and this scale had ever been seen in the United Kingdom before. London put into the field at one time 20,000 soldiers and 8,000 armed police. Bombs, machine-guns, rocket launchers, land mines and Semtex high explosive took many lives and did immense damage to property. It is estimated that 3,500 were killed and 30,000 injured in the carnage. Those trying to bring about security lost 300 officers dead and 9,000 wounded.

Myth, almost certainly, injected an element of fatalism into the situation. The IRA seldom lost an opportunity to put into

words its dream of eventual and certain success. Their right to fight and to
march through disputed streets was
sacrosanct. If taken prisoner they
might starve themselves to death. Those who sacrificed themselves were heroes. Myths and memories mobilized those
fighting for liberation and consolidated their resolve. Terror
methods were regrettable but perhaps indispensable. They
were never, of course, calling themselves terrorists.

TERROR METHODS WERE REGRETTABLE BUT PERHAPS INDISPENSABLE.

Moves to end the time of terror have been many and various,
involving London, Belfast, Dublin, and US presidents. Early
attempts to take a tough stance towards insurrection were
summary arrest, internment, and direct rule by Whitehall.
Not one of these steps ended the conflict. It was after 1993
that intensive exploratory talks and pencilled-in agreements
opened up the prospect of peace at last. Unionists raged about
British ministers 'conniving' with terrorists. A breakthrough
came in April 1998 with the Good Friday Agreement to ini-
tiate a 'peace process'. After thirty years of strife, surely, was
this the beginning of the end of violence? Seven out of ten
people in the Province of Northern Ireland expressed their
fervent hope that it would be so.

While the heat of confrontation and the use of lethal
weaponry has diminished not quite to vanishing point but to
a very low level of intensity there remain grave hindrances to
a terror-free Northern Ireland. In the first place, there has
been a splintering of the rival fronts to form 'paramilitary'
units. Catholic activists are now to be found variously in the
Provisional IRA, the Official IRA, The Continuity IRA, the

THERE HAS BEEN A SPLINTERING OF THE RIVAL FRONTS TO FORM 'PARAMILITARY' UNITS. Dissident IRA, the Real IRA, the Catholic Reaction Force, and the Irish National Liberation Army. The very names are significant (and provocative to opponents) and while it would not be right in general to call these activists terrorists there is the potential here for resumption of violent tactics. Indeed, it is the Real IRA that have admitted attempts at bombing on the British mainland in 2000 and 2001. Pitted against these Republican groups is an array of Protestants who wear the badges of Ulster Unionists, the Ulster Volunteer Force, the Loyalist Ulster Volunteer Force, the Ulster Freedom Fighters (Ulster Defence Association), the Orange Volunteers and the Red Hand Defenders. The last two bands were proscribed by the government in 1999.

A second hindrance to a terrorist-free community has been reluctance to disarm. Much official enquiry since 1996 confirms that weapon stocks in numerous sectarian hands are still substantial. In July 2005, IRA leaders ordered members to stop their armed campaign. 'Exclusively peaceful means' were to be employed henceforth. On all sides there was a call for the IRA to be disbanded. In late September, the head of the arms decommissioning body reported that arms had been 'put beyond use'. The situation continues to be carefully monitored by the British government, with some of the arsenals investigated and reserves destroyed. However, there are obstacles to progress. Some wings of the IRA, 'marking time' as it were, see the handing in of arms as 'surrender'. There are those in Sinn Fein who want a much fairer political deal before they will hand in means of effective defence. On the other side, there are Unionists who will have absolutely no dealings with 'terrorists'. For them, the real terrorists sit in Northern Ireland's coalition administration at Stormont. The African National Congress in South Africa and the Palestine Liberation Organization in the Middle East faced similar demands for disarmament, and objections about it, and the matter was resolved through carefully phased partial and then entire arms surrender which was not to be seen as political surrender.

Thus, in Northern Ireland, as in Spain, we have beliefs and hopes and terrorism all in a state of suspense. As in Spain, there are questions about terrorism's persistence and about its utility. A US senator, painfully mediating in Belfast, put the need very directly in

WE WOULD NEVER GET RID OF TERRORISM UNLESS THERE WAS A DECOMMISSIONING OF 'MINDSETS'.

1999. Decommissioning of weapons was vital to the resto-
ration of peace but we would never get rid of terrorism unless there was a decommissioning of 'mindsets', that is, attitudes and prejudices.

Attempts to clear minds on these lines are now being objectively pursued among cross-party volunteer groups in today's Northern Ireland.

In official circles the Northern Ireland Assembly remains sus-
pended since October 2002 and direct rule from London is still in place. In the four years since then Whitehall has assumed responsibility for the 'marching season', and arrangements for compensating terrorism's victims. Prime ministers

Box 2

A terrorist incident

Place

Over Lockerbie, south-west Scotland, 21 December 1988

Incident

- A bomb placed in a radio-cassette believed loaded at Frankfurt and reloaded at London flight change.
- Pan Am flight for the United States exploded mid-air.
- All 259 passengers died, and 11 Scots on the ground.

Consequences

- British/US enquiries indicted Abel Basut al-Maghrahi (Center of Strategic Studies, Tripoli, Libya) and Laman Khalifa Fhimah (director, Libya Airline, Malta) as apparently responsible for bombing. Had trained in Libya 3 years.
- United States demanded suspects' extradition; Security Council Resolution supported.
- United States, Britain and others banned Libya Airline connections, drastically reduced oil sales, imposed trade sanctions, banned Libyan diplomats.
- Quaddafi humiliated.
- Libya in 1999 agreed extradition to Scottish law trial in Netherlands (temporarily part of Scotland). Three Scots judges found Maghrahi guilty, gave life-sentence, Fhimah acquitted, returned to welcome in Tripoli.
- Maghrahi appeal to be heard, January 2002, on grounds circumstantial evidence disputed. Appeal dismissed March 2002.

from London and Dublin regularly confer and commute to the troubled province in a purposeful attempt to hoist into place lasting peace and security. They now have in mind the re-establishment of a power-sharing assembly within a span of six months. Rhetoric resounds in Belfast, as it does in Madrid and Colombo, talking of a future of 'togetherness' to displace fratricide. On the ground, though, where isolated terrorist incidents crop up occasionally, progress is sadly slow moving.

THE AMERICAS: PERU

Another example of terrorism in suspense is in Peru. The scenario there is unlike any other, and puzzling. If Algeria is said to be the world's most dangerous place then Peru comes high on the list afterwards. The Shining Path (Sendero Luminoso) of Peru is thought

THE SHINING PATH OF PERU IS THOUGHT TO BE THE MOST DANGEROUS OF TERRORIST GROUPS.

to be the most dangerous of terrorist groups. It has been a menace to ordered living for three decades.

Nobody would have imagined that a cluster of young professors in a rural university in Peru would ever launch a vicious campaign of terror. Their objective in 1963 was the thoroughly creditable one of reinvigorating poor Indian villagers by means of hands-on skills training, family case work, medical research, welfare projects and teacher training. It is true that idealists among them had Marxist and Maoist leanings, nevertheless, they found it easy and necessary to work in tandem with the government in Lima. After an encouraging start, a number of the academics leading the enterprise began to assert, rather impatiently, that a reasonable deal for poor peasants depended upon a wholesale transformation of both government and society. This notion of revolution, though peaceful enough, sufficed to frighten the Peruvian government by the mid-1970s. The robust tactics they used to contain revolt only made the dissidents bolder. Their educational extension movement, the Shining Path to the Future, the path of peace, was now by way of becoming the Shining Path of a people's war. Consequently, several things happened. First, recruits were enlisted and armed as a revolutionary spearhead. Ten thousand frontline fighters felt they could rely on five times as many sympathizers. Next, an elaborate organization was devised to provide cells of partisans, men and women, masked and unknown to each other, who were to disperse into selected strongholds. Regional committees were told to coordinate a strategy of containment, attack and annihilation. Shining Path had become a sect, dedicated almost in a quasi-religious sense to terrorism (though its disciples would deny the label) and with the original leader, Professor Guzman, as its messiah. Nothing was to be left to chance. From being a movement for the people, Shining Path swerved sideways into war against the people. Their motto put it graphically, namely, that everything other than power for the Party and its clique of founders was an illusion. Reality would soon extinguish people who were content with illusions. The gruesome result of what appeared to be terrorism going mad was the death of at least 30,000 Peruvians, and some 3,000 who had 'disappeared'. At least 2,500 terrorists were rounded up for execution.

Today, the majority of Peruvians wring their hands over the fear and uncertainty that terrorism in suspense has brought to their land. Guzman himself has been imprisoned, sentenced to life imprisonment. Shining Path remains a menace partly because it is

THERE IS NO SHORTAGE OF UNEMPLOYED TEENAGERS TO JOIN THE RANKS OF SOMETHING LIKE 200 MASKED, HEAVILY ARMED TERRORISTS.

self-sufficient, 'living off the land' that terrified peasants own and till. Violent activity is financed by bank robbery and a carefully maintained 'protection' racket. There is no shortage of unemployed teenagers to join the ranks of something like 200 masked, heavily armed terrorists. There is every reason to suppose that the followers of Shining Path are waiting in the wings for any opportunity to demonstrate that violence may not win a cause but it does not necessarily lose one.

There are other terrorist groups in Latin America, though none so formidable or so lasting a menace as Peru's Shining Path. The picture is a shadowy one, with organizations dynamic in leadership and consistent in strategy, which have been 'in business' for some years. There are also small groups with shifting motives, management and numbers, 'men of the moment' whose ardour may arise and vanish as political circumstances change. Contemporary groups, violent enough to worry governments, are, in Chile, the Lautaro Youth Movement (LVF) and the Manuel Rodriguez Patriotic Front (FPMR), in Colombia, the National Liberation Army (ELN) and the Revolutionary Armed Front of Colombia (FARC), in Bolivia, the Nestor Paz Zamora Commission (CNPZ) and, in Peru, as well as Shining Path, the Tupac Amaru Revolutionary Movement (MRTA).

chapter four

MOTIVES FOR
TERRORISM

After the horrific bombing in New York and Washington on 11 September 2001, there were questions in everybody's minds. Why did those terrorists do what they did? What possible motive could they have had? Were they absolutely insane? Could the incidents have been planned long beforehand in minute detail? The Pentagon in Washington was a military objective and a tempting one for those who wanted to disable the United States. The World Trade Center, though – how is it that those innocent workers there from many lands were victims of some dreadful plot?

Similar questions can be heard from time to time in places as diverse as Bethlehem, London, Jerusalem, Istanbul, Madrid, Moscow, places where terrorism has cost lives and property. It is understandable that such questions are a predictable response to grief and anger. When the identity of terrorists is revealed, either through their defiant challenge or as a result of forensic investigation, the reader or onlooker usually concludes that what has happened is not unexpected because of what we think we know about the terrorists' intentions. To leave a bomb in a car, to rake a market crowd with a machine-gun, to blow up a plane – these are major examples of violence gone berserk, we say. The 'game-plan' has really gone too far. The incidents which involve personal injury such as 'kneecapping' in Northern Ireland or 'necklacing', as it was practised in apartheid South Africa, appear to raise rather different questions when we wonder about the sheer evil of the perpetrator.

TERRORIST MOTIVES: A FIRST ATTEMPT TO UNDERSTAND THEM

It seems to be part of a sense of shock and disgust and incredulity that the questions when asked are generally followed by swift condemnation. 'When is a terrorist not a terrorist? When he's a dead one', was a question-with-answer frequently heard among British troops in 1950 sent to Malaya to put down a Communist and

'WHEN IS A TERRORIST NOT A TERRORIST? WHEN HE'S A DEAD ONE'

nationalist insurrection. It may even be thought disloyal and unpatriotic to stand back and conjecture too much. Terrorists are insane and inhuman. Can their motives be thought of as rational or calculated? And if it is possible to work out their likely motives are these not so inexcusable that retaliation must be our prime consideration? It is always important to stress that our attempts to understand terrorist motives are mainly based on assumptions. Terrorists are unlikely to volunteer to be interviewed.

Where terror methods are acknowledged to be the last resort, say, of those fighting for freedom the question as to motive answers itself and there may be widespread sympathy. Violence may not be condoned but be thought inevitable. Thus, as an earlier chapter has remarked, the arduous, defensive struggle of the resistance and of partisans during the Second World War was generally admired even though many of their offensive methods were cruel and often indiscriminate. The flush of anti-colonial liberation movements soon after 1945 gained support from many nations. The wish to be rid of apartheid was strongly supported by liberals around the world. The basic fight by the African National Congress and others for liberty and independence was seen in these instances to be a leading motive except that if it led to sustained violence and, worse still, to civil war, there was much less approval in other quarters. In numerous former imperial territories such as Cyprus, India, Malaya, Kenya, Burma and Indonesia, nationalist campaigning soon broke down into large-scale violence where the original motives became twisted and chaotic.

TERRORIST MOTIVES ON FURTHER REFLECTION

Terrorists, these days, are generally considered to be rational in their beliefs and in their behaviour. They certainly claim to be. Occasionally there will be random, impulsive acts of destruction, those that hit the headlines, but the evidence points to individuals, usually members of groups, thinking out their objectives and then carefully planning how best to achieve them. After all, a widely accepted definition of terrorism, readers will recall, is that it is a premeditated threat or use of violence with the intention of intimidating the authorities. The terrorist will draw up a list of objectives. His general approach, weighing up the possibilities, calculating the risks, choosing options, thinking about when and where it is best to act, this is his strategy. More detailed planning goes into tactics. Who is to do what? How many people will be required? What methods are to be used? How do we set about the project? What about the security of the place we shall visit? How do we get away afterwards? Motives start out by being political or ideological or religious: they are soon translated into intentions and behaviour. They may not always result in violence. Again, many terrorists who do not want to be labelled in that way will also stress that it was not they who chose violence: it was the unreasonableness (or something else) of the opposition.

A good deal has been written about the circumstances that make the road to violence the only way out of despair. A brief discussion will have to suffice on this occasion. The root of that dissatisfaction may be oppression by a military regime, as in Argentina, or the prejudice and hostility of a majority who make living by a minority insufferable, as it was in the Balkans for Muslims or in Iraq for Kurds. In many Latin American states, Peru, Uruguay, Chile and Colombia, there was gross lack of opportunity both for workers and the middle class in towns and for peasants in the countryside. Protest demonstrations were brutally put down and violence erupted in a way that the first hopes and visions of reformers could not stem. Ultimately, for those who would like to move peacefully and intelligibly, options become narrower and narrower.

ULTIMATELY, FOR THOSE WHO WOULD LIKE TO MOVE PEACEFULLY AND INTELLIGIBLY, OPTIONS BECOME NARROWER AND NARROWER.

The only way forward is the way of strength and that will involve risks and loss and suffering. For the young who are unsuccessful and disenchanted by life in big cities or in back-of-beyond rural settlements there is the way of protest either through individual deviance or through enrolling in some sort of group which sets itself up against the authorities, their representatives or their allies. Most of us tend to be judgemental about 'hooligans' or 'lager louts' without perhaps understanding that their aggressive behaviour may well be orchestrated and scaled up into those crowds of Palestinian youth throwing rocks in the *intifada* or the ranks of young Irishmen setting vehicles and buildings alight in Londonderry or North Belfast. To be a member of a group of others that does something active is a powerful motive and most terrorist groups have little difficulty in recruiting angry young men and women.

A PRELUDE TO ACTION

What was in the mind of the terrorists who carried out incidents that everyone remembers with horror? The capture and murder of Italy's former Prime Minister, Aldo Moro, in 1984, bombs in London in 1984, 1996, 2000 and 2005, the blowing apart of a bus in Jerusalem in 1996, and in 1998 the blasting of US embassies in Kenya and Tanzania and the kidnap of sixteen Western tourists in Yemen. Then, apart from the mayhem in New York and Washington in September 2001 where the intentions of the terrorists are still a matter for speculation, there are the lone 'Unabomber' Kaczynski of 1995 and in the same year Timothy McVeigh with his destruction of a Federal Office building in Oklahoma City.

Investigation of these incidents and a host of others points to a number of likely motives. There is, as mainspring, the notion that a power-change is the major objective. Undoubtedly, a clique with action in mind will see situations and people in terms of 'Us' and 'Them', or good as opposed to evil. In other words, We are Right and They are Wrong and They must be Removed. Apart from a definite goal and a necessary target, group cohesiveness is the vital component in order for the group to succeed. This is seen clearly in groups where members have the same ethnic origins as with the Palestinians, or the Hizbullah, or the Basques, or if there is a religious dedication or a shared language. Equally compelling as an incentive to work closely together will be intolerance and discrimination from 'outside'. In the interests of consolidating the group, loyalty is an absolute requirement, loyalty pushed to the extreme of sacrifice. There is no room for argument about motives, no possibility of compromise, for that would break the group cohesion. For the terrorists a strong leader, admired and obeyed, is a real necessity. The terrorist learns by doing, not by any book. (A point here is that Muslim terrorists, in fact, grievously offend against their sacred book, the Koran, and its express prohibition of violence directed against others.) No Geneva Conventions prohibit the nature and extent of what modern terrorists may decide to do because the Conventions were designed for 'orderly' warfare between sovereign states. Modern terrorism in some respects is more violent than ever if its agents decide to destroy an aircraft and can take 200 or more lives at one blow. Urban terrorism is able also to cause significant damage if the motive includes slaughter in a crowded city or extensive damage to buildings and infrastructure. More targets are possible and there may be less risk to terrorists. Although the planning of an incident clearly must be done in secret, the incident itself will yield plenty of publicity when modern information technology is used and the violence itself attracts media attention. Publicity for terrorism, when it revitalizes the

PUBLICITY FOR TERRORISM, WHEN IT REVITALIZES THE TERRORISTS, HAS BEEN TERMED 'OXYGEN'.

terrorists, has been termed 'oxygen'. Security authorities are, of course, also using sophisticated technology to track down conspirators. Before any terrorist attack is mounted, success must be weighed against the possibility of detection and prevention. A realistic balance of benefits and costs will have to appraise as accurately as possible the state of readiness of the authority's security arrangements. There is always, one would suppose, the idea that a group keeps further violence in reserve if their demands are not met. The previous chapter described the situation in Basque Spain, in Northern Ireland and in Peru as 'suspended terrorism'.

TERRORIST MOTIVES IN CONTEXT

Motives should not be discussed without looking carefully at the contexts in which they are meaningful. The last chapter did take some account of motivation in the case of the terrorist groups described and a number of the methods that such groups use will be listed in Chapter 7. For the moment it might be helpful to set the motives that we have already mentioned in the context of where and when they appear to have been responsible for terrorist action.

Basques and Tamils

As most terrorists see it, their struggle for power is a consequence of their being denied adequate representation or opportunity. The Basques in

THE BASQUES IN SPAIN AND THE TAMILS IN SRI LANKA SHARE THE NOTION THAT THEY HAVE NO POWER BASE, NO ACKNOWLEDGEMENT OF THEIR CULTURAL DISTINCTIVENESS, AND THAT THEY ARE BEING DISCRIMINATED AGAINST.

Spain and the Tamils in Sri Lanka share the notion that they have no power base, no acknowledgement of their cultural distinctiveness, and that they are being discriminated against. Both wage an unremitting battle to make their case to those they regard as oppressors. Both stress togetherness, since to demonstrate that you have a unified cause must depend upon your cohesiveness and your preparedness to defend it. From the outside, there is a similarity in a contest which deteriorates into violence and terrorism. There the similarity ends for the context reveals the contrast between Spain and Sri Lanka and that makes generalizing without looking most carefully at the context both unhelpful and misleading. As we have seen earlier, terrorist motives may be shelved and suspended for the time being either if the going gets too hard or if the other side arranges terms of agreement and a ceasefire which seems to protestors only a temporary and scarcely satisfactory measure. This has happened in the case of ETA and the IRA. There is a publicity bonus here if in the media and among the public at large there is a continuing debate and a good deal of uncertainty and fear.

PLO and IRA

At first glance, there appears to be something similar in the motives associated with the PLO and the IRA during the years 1991 to the end of the century. There is with both groups an apparent two-way move preferring negotiation to outright fighting yet with a suspended or randomly active military wing. Again, in each case, the political front is concerned to hammer out guarantees and to make concessions while the armed men in the background display evident reluctance to 'sacrifice' what the use of weapons and their steely resolve gained for them. In the case of Northern Ireland, the unreadiness of the military wing to give up its eagerness to use force was made more obvious when it began to split into rival sub-groups. Publicity has been all-important for the Palestinians and for the IRA as it has been for most terrorists, in that it lends a focus to their aspirations and activities, consolidates their sense of mission, and helps to bring along willing recruits. Publicity works in more than one way, however. Conspirators hope that media coverage of their terror tactics will force a government to the negotiating table. That may well be so but if bombs and massacres are still pictured on television this will inevitably harden public attitudes.

CONSPIRATORS HOPE THAT MEDIA COVERAGE OF THEIR TERROR TACTICS WILL FORCE A GOVERNMENT TO THE NEGOTIATING TABLE.

Peru's Shining Path

Nowhere is a consideration of terrorist motives more intriguing than in the instance of the Shining Path movement in Peru. As we have already seen, there was a transformation, with the original visions of the founders, meant to be constructive and educational, sheering away into ideological narrowness, and worse still into destructive impulses. An obsession with personal power turned into hatred of any opposition. To this was added corruption, intrigue, enmity and death. The concern to build cohesion, which is so marked with other groups, became tainted with what its critics termed 'fascism'. The context within which terrorism still operates spasmodically in Peru is a thoroughly nihilistic one since it is difficult to see a benefit to anyone from what appear to be poisonous motives.

Libya

An earlier chapter has described a dramatic change in Libya's motives. Colonel Quaddafi and his associates, with their original drive for unity at all costs together with a penetrating sense of religious mission, convinced the rest of the world that they were a nation inciting revolution and perfecting aggressive techniques 'by the people and for the people'. The techniques were to be branded as Libyan and exported by an unscrupulous regime as a means of state-sponsored subversion, terror and destruction. By 1990 Libyan perspectives were changing. International counter-terrorism, by way of military reprisals and economic sanctions, was never wholly effective in diminishing terrorist activity by Libya but it increasingly began to dull the edge of terrorist zeal. More tempting were the allurements of a Western world's need of dependable oil supplies. The motives of Libyans which led to the adoption of terror tactics were gradually being displaced by more peaceful commercial and diplomatic interests.

> **COLONEL QUADDAFI AND HIS ASSOCIATES CONVINCED THE REST OF THE WORLD THAT THEY WERE A NATION INCITING REVOLUTION AND PERFECTING AGGRESSIVE TECHNIQUES 'BY THE PEOPLE AND FOR THE PEOPLE'.**

WHO BECOMES A TERRORIST?

The individual recruit

Speculation about the kind of people who become involved in terrorism is common and tempting. Sociologists, psychologists, criminologists and others have shown an interest in this question for a long time, but few definite conclusions have been reached. One can say with some certainty that the causes of terrorism lie both within the individual, the group he or she joins, and the nature of the larger society in which terrorism develops. Tensions and difficulties may exist in all these areas and play a part in the choices an individual makes. There are social psychologists, for instance, Albert Bandura, who think that joining a terrorist group in the case of an individual may just be due to a 'Chance Life Encounter'. It is not always careful thinking about causes and consequences that leads to their decision to join a terrorist group.

A study of how terrorist groups recruit new members would be revealing and interesting, giving us some answers, but facts about successful recruitment are **FACTS ABOUT SUCCESSFUL RECRUITMENT ARE HARD TO COME BY.** hard to come by. There is not much we can do other than to proceed by way of using assumptions, bearing in mind the uniqueness of the individual and the diversity of human groups. There will always be exceptions.

There is a general consensus about many aspects of the recruits. Many of them are young adolescents, sometimes from broken families, who may not have been very successful in their lives so far. They may feel alienated, outsiders in the communities in which they live. Adolescence is, as we know, a time for rebellion against established values in home and society and opposition to authority in general, but in many cases the difficulties lie deeper. Their self-image and self-confidence is often weak and they are susceptible to pressures from others and perhaps to political and religious indoctrination.

The outstanding common characteristic of members of terrorist groups, so researchers declare, is their normality. They are not generally psychopaths, nor are they suffering from any particular mental disorder. Diverse types of personality appear to be attracted by terrorism and their motives may be very different but certain personality traits are common. These young people are often 'action-oriented', aggressive, hungry for stimuli of various sorts and keen to seek excitement. Those who come from the margins of society find for the first time in their lives that they now really 'belong'. It is what they can now do that matters. Very seldom are they searching within themselves for the reasons for earlier failures. Unable to face up to their own sense of inadequacy, they will blame others, the establishment, the state, for problems that are of others' making. Scapegoats will be found. Like the often-criticized 'hoodlum' they may crave and find an outlet for anger, perhaps hatred, and often violence.

THOSE WHO COME FROM THE MARGINS OF SOCIETY FIND FOR THE FIRST TIME IN THEIR LIVES THAT THEY NOW REALLY 'BELONG'.

The group

Usually, the members of a terrorist group change considerably once they have joined. This process of transition is in the field of group dynamics. Sociologists such as W. R. Bion, in 1961, have described how members of a group are encouraged to submerge their individual identities, to subscribe to the rules, moral codes and motives of their host group. This happens in gangs and cults all over the world. The individual, in 'belonging', is offered a chance of action and accepts the dictates of leader and fellow members. Bion, in his

THE INDIVIDUAL, IN 'BELONGING', IS OFFERED A CHANCE OF ACTION AND ACCEPTS THE DICTATES OF LEADER AND FELLOW MEMBERS.

account of group dynamics, has the leader in the role of he who decides the motive for action. In line with motives and after calculating the odds, the further move of the group may be either 'fight' or 'flight'. The leader's decision will justify the methods to be used and the choice of victim. Not one of the members is likely to show disloyalty and risk their membership by openly questioning either the leader or what they understand to be the consensus of an authoritarian group committed to certain methods and objectives. Under such influences, violence becomes easy to accept by those who maybe would never have chosen it alone.

After a while the members are unable to leave the group which has become their sole source of support. An American professor of psychiatry, Jerrold M. Post, writing in 1990 about

DOUBTS ABOUT THE LEGITIMACY OF GOALS AND ACTIONS ARE INTOLERABLE TO A GROUP.

group survival and dismissal, sees doubts about the legitimacy of goals and actions as intolerable to a group. Indeed, withdrawal is impossible, 'except by way of the graveyard'. The way to get rid of doubt is to 'get rid of the doubters'. The values and moral codes learned before joining the group fade. A motive for a terrorist attack which might once have appalled a young recruit is now understandable and pardonable because it is pronounced by the leader and sanctioned by the others. Post gives an example from post-war Germany and its Red Army Faction terrorist group, when a young recruit was told of a plan to firebomb a store. Horrified, the recruit blurted out, 'But that will lead to the loss of innocent lives!' There was an ice-cold reaction to this from comrades who now grimly questioned his motives, reliability and membership. At all costs the group must go on, cannot give up, must act to justify its very existence. Members leaving the group would collapse both the group and their own sense of self-esteem. Outside the group nobody can see the sense of the Basque ETA, and the Tamil Tigers, pursuing their campaign of violence when much of what they are wanting has been given them through compromise, agreement or grant of more autonomy. Their subsidiary motives of targeting people and places become subsumed in a narrow, ultimate motive of ensuring survival. Whatever the degree of risk (and the irritated bewilderment of everybody else) the terrorists continue to terrorize.

How, then, does anyone outside a terrorist group help it to disband? Jerrold Post concludes that there are, in fact, possibilities. We should start at the beginning by thinking back to reasons why individuals in particular places feel so inadequate and alienated that they cannot resist the allurement of a violent group. There is a need to dissuade likely recruits. In some careful way, alternative 'paths out' must be provided to facilitate leaving. Can we make available more personal security, more tangible benefits, encourage more credible motives, and far more opportunities in the long term? And more widely, there has to be a programme for reducing public sympathy and support. This is a tall order and stuff for extensive debate as to how it should be done and who would attempt to do it.

THE LONE TERRORIST

So far it is group motivation that has been discussed. A last question is to do with the motives that very likely determine or influence what a terrorist does acting in isolation. Two examples of this troubled the United States in the summer of 1995. In June that year a number of Californians, working in universities or for airline companies, received through the post packets containing simple but deadly bombs. Three of them died and twenty-three were injured as a result of this. The mailing of these packets was traced back to Theodore Kaczynski, a professor of mathematics, but at an early stage in the investigation and before an arrest could be made Kaczynski had offered to stop what he was doing, provided a number of US newspapers would print a long article of his which deplored environmental exploitation and pollution. This terrorist's motives were clearly very much mixed but his desire for publicity was to bring him to book and he was arrested. Frustration and loneliness pushed him towards murderous intent.

The other outrage of dramatic proportions also in 1995 was the bombing of an important state building in Oklahoma City (see Box 3). For this, a Vietnam veteran, Timothy McVeigh, was indicted, although taking him to trial occupied two years. Once more the basic feelings of frustration and loneliness were at the heart of a personality that had been attracted to the white supremacy movement in the United States, a movement much more vicious and more powerful than the Klu Klux Klan. McVeigh wanted revenge for what he sensed were the multicultural liberal policies of the Clinton Administration.

MCVEIGH WANTED REVENGE FOR WHAT HE SENSED WERE THE MULTICULTURAL LIBERAL POLICIES OF THE CLINTON ADMINISTRATION.

His interest in the liaisons between fundamentalist religious sects and the 'gun lobby' led to no regrets at taking 168 lives to advance a cause. What these examples do show is that in a democracy where free speech and reasonable protests are allowable, it is not easy to determine just how far this freedom permits an individual's motives to become incentives for dangerous and anti-social behaviour, the roots of terrorism.

One of the strongest motivating forces in terrorism has always been religious zeal, especially when it can be said to have such a strong, orthodox component that it narrows observance and is intolerant of any deviation, let alone heresy. The links between religion and terrorism will be discussed in Chapter 5.

Box 3

A terrorist incident

Place

Oklahoma City, United States, 19 April 1995

Incident

- Explosion devastated Alfred P. Murrah Federal Building downtown.
- 168 died including 19 children. More than 400 injured.
- Timothy McVeigh arrested for traffic offence, later arrested as bombing suspect, charged.
- Accomplice Terry Nichols arrested. McVeigh and Nichols identified as right-wing, white supremacist group members.

Consequences

- Trial moved to Denver to ensure fairer, safer trial.
- June 1997 – McVeigh found guilty on 11 counts.
- December 1997 – Nichols found guilty of involuntary manslaughter, conspiracy with McVeigh.
- May 1998 – Nichols given life sentence.
- March 1999 – McVeigh appeal rejected.
- October 2000 – Request for new McVeigh trial rejected.
- June 2001 – McVeigh executed. Sorry for sufferers but no regrets about 'military action' against 'over-reaching' government.
- Continuing debate in United States: does McVeigh death sentence, and execution, make him a martyr? Alternative of life sentence?

chapter five

TERRORISM AND RELIGION

Religion and terrorism go hand in hand – in some places and among some people. Readers of newspapers and television viewers can be forgiven for coming to that conclusion. Are religious impulses often a driving force among terrorists? Consider this list of serious terrorist incidents for just six years, 1992–98:

- 1992   Algeria – Muslim extremists burn villages, restaurants, markets.
- 1993   Bombay – Muslim gangs kill Hindus for destroying a Muslim temple.
- 1994   Jerusalem – An ultranationalist Jew enters an Islamic mosque and kills 29 at prayer.
- 1995   Jerusalem – Israeli ex-premier, Yitzhak Rabin, shot by Orthodox youth.
- 1995   Oklahoma – federal building bombed by Christian Patriots and 168 die.
- 1995   Tokyo – nerve gas attack by religious sect, 12 die, 3,700 injured.
- 1996   Saudi Arabia – US Air Force barracks torched – by Saudi religious cult.
- 1996   Luxor – Muslim Brotherhood shoot 50 foreign tourists.
- 1996   Jerusalem – Hamas suicide members kill more than 60 Israelis.
- 1998   Nairobi and Dar es Salaam – al-Qaida (Islamic members) bomb US embassies killing 224.

It looks as though religious influences were a driving force on these occasions. Are there, then, aspects of religious belief and of believers that lend themselves to expression through the use of force? Certain religions, for example, Christianity and Islam, share a number of characteristics:

- an obligation to worship and obey one Divine Being
- a code of belief which should be unhesitatingly followed and practised
- indoctrination ensures that faith is reinforced and that actions undergird it
- the institution of a leader or leaders who expect loyal support from 'the faithful'
- individual followers, taught the difference between 'right' and 'wrong' must strive unceasingly to observe that difference and reject all alternatives
- failure to follow the code or, even worse, heresy, means punishment
- the blessed receive a reward after death (Paradise): the wicked will suffer torment
- those who remain faithful to the code are loyal to a 'community of believers'.

It is not difficult to see that religious influences and expectations help to build resolve and unity, a sense of rightness, possibly uniqueness, and the hope of reward. Solidarity formed in these ways may lead to all things good. The idea is there of a duty to go out and convert others. If unity leads to intolerance towards others, the consequences may be discrimination, persecution and even violent action. Few of us would want to link religious belief and observance with anything harmful to others but the tally of incidents listed above and the possible impulses among the terrorists concerned (in the light of their religious upbringing) all make for some worrying thoughts about motivation.

TERRORISM AND ISLAM

There is now a more pronounced religious element to international terrorism than there ever was in the last century.

Bruce Hoffman, renowned expert on international terrorism, has estimated that nearly half of the number of today's terrorist groups could be classified as religious in character and/or motivation. Much of it

NEARLY HALF OF THE NUMBER OF TODAY'S TERRORIST GROUPS COULD BE CLASSIFIED AS RELIGIOUS IN CHARACTER AND/OR MOTIVATION.

could be seen as a result of the spectacular revolution in Iran in 1979 which so dramatically demonstrated the decisive zeal and forcefulness of Islamic reformers. Throughout the Middle East, especially, there has been a cycle of protest and revolutionary action from Algiers to Beirut and Tel Aviv. Most ominously for world peace, there has been a deliberate export of terrorists, whose religious affiliation cannot be denied, from Arab lands to Europe, Asia and North America. Fanatics and martyrs are everywhere as the next chapter will relate.

It is unfortunate that terrorism is more marked in places where the major religion is that of Islam. That fact has had something to do with the steady stream of books that associate Islam with militancy, fear and violent aggression towards 'infidels'. Contents in many of these books and in the popular media frequently lean towards half-truths and misinformation. It is true that Washington has labelled five Middle Eastern states as inclined towards terrorism although the evidence is not all that reliable. However, Islam's official voices were quick to pass on condolences to an anguished United States on 11 September. It is equally true that among the 1.3 billion Muslims in the world, that is, one in five of us, there has been much unhappiness and resentment over the American military strikes in Afghanistan.

There are one or two aspects of religious belief among Muslims that could give rise to some anxiety among 'outsiders'. Islam does have certain beliefs and practices reinforcing it as a way of life in contrast to take-it-or-leave-it Christianity. At heart, the Muslim is not violent. He is an idealist, commanded by the Koran, the writings of the Prophet Mohammed, 1,400 years ago, to live truthfully, honestly, and to respect all others. He treads the Right Path peacefully to acknowledge the unity and equality of mankind. However, truth and rightness must win over rebellion and lack of faith. A devout Muslim must be prepared to embark upon a jihad, a struggle for self-improvement but also a prime duty to go out and defend the 'holiness' of Islam. That can have a political as well as religious meaning – the land and the faith are sacred. Those who would oppose are enemies. Thus, we have here a potential springboard for 'acting-out', violent or not violent.

THE MUSLIM IS AN IDEALIST, COMMANDED BY THE KORAN, TO LIVE TRUTHFULLY, HONESTLY, AND TO RESPECT ALL OTHERS.

A misunderstanding recently has been the gloss placed on the writing of Harvard Professor Samuel P. Huntingdon, the 'clash of civilizations man', much quoted in today's news and comment. What Huntingdon did suggest, perhaps a little too hastily, was that we are now in an era of Muslim wars. Muslims are fighting Muslims in two out of three of the world's present thirty-two conflicts. There are terrorist incidents, guerrilla campaigns, civil wars, and interstate wars. A Muslim-influenced conflict was sprung on New York and Washington on 11 September 2001. There could well be an inescapable confrontation of East and West and in that

MUSLIMS ARE FIGHTING MUSLIMS IN TWO OUT OF THREE OF THE WORLD'S PRESENT THIRTY-TWO CONFLICTS.

sense a clash of rival cultures and civilizations. Not necessarily so, though; more likely is a series of violent episodes, dispersed, varied and frequent. Terrorists will be able to stage politico-religious scenarios. Hostility towards the 'imperialist' West is already smouldering among that great reservoir of activists, the young unemployed of sixteen to thirty years.

A feature of contemporary Islam, and something that worries many in Islam and observers elsewhere, is the rapid growth of fundamentalism in the Middle East. Muslims who belong to this creed are the most intolerant members of any religion. Their narrow-mindedness renders them incapable of any agreement or compromise with those who think differently. Characteristics common to many more moderate religions have already been outlined but looking at them as they might be interpreted by fundamentalist believers the potential for aggressive action is there:

- An inner 'voice of God' requires unquestioning obedience and fanatical devotion.

- The code of the Koran and the rigid Shari'ah code of conduct are to be observed so strictly that unbelievers, infidels, or followers of the Great Satan are to be rejected and conquered. Their destruction becomes a sacred duty and a crusade.

- The Will of God and the doctrine of the Koran make our actions legitimate, however unrestrained and violent they may be.

- Our leaders in belief (or in the field) will be given undying respect and loyalty.

- Failure to carry out a mission or to be tempted by heresy is unpardonable.

- The faithful will receive final reward but only if they remain absolutely steadfast.

Even the briefest consideration of religious aspects such as these, and they are largely Islamic, points to their observance making for ruthless moves against anyone else. If, added to religious zeal on this scale, there is political grievance and contest, say, between Palestinian Arabs and Israelis, or between the underprivileged in Egypt, Algeria, Iran and the exploiting, capitalist West, then the bullet and the bomb may be enlisted to settle

IF, ADDED TO RELIGIOUS ZEAL ON THIS SCALE, THERE IS POLITICAL GRIEVANCE AND CONTEST, THEN THE BULLET AND THE BOMB MAY BE ENLISTED TO SETTLE DIFFERENCES.

differences. Fundamentalist beliefs seem at their strongest among the working masses in the more backward regions of the Arab world for they are the ones feeling alienated, turned in upon themselves, and resentful, no doubt, that the promises of a better future, this side of Heaven, are seldom made real. Their frustration, if it is there, can be orchestrated by propaganda and agitators. For a tiny minority of extremists among them it may be necessary to find a scapegoat and to learn how to savage it.

AL-QAIDA AND THE TALIBAN

Whether or not one goes along with the idea that religion may fuel terrorist activity, it is useful to look at the makeup of some of the most zealous groups. In this chapter, there is a focus on al-Qaida, the group that everybody was talking about in 2001. Very thorough investigation in the United States had already identified al-Qaida in the 1990s as a desperate terrorist enterprise, with satellite cells in numerous countries, which was almost certainly responsible for a chain of terrorist atrocities, notably, the East African embassy bombings of 1998 and the destruction of the World Trade Center on 11 September 2001. In American eyes, al-Qaida must have had a lot to do with the fact that one in three international ter-rorist attacks was being directed at American interests. An angry and anguished Washington then decided to mount military strikes to punish those held to be responsible for the incidents, and to prevent their doing anything like that again. Two other matters concerned the United States and the other nations that were consulted about the response. Most of all, al-Qaida was being given sanctuary by a funda-mentalist regime, known as Taliban in Afghanistan. Taliban had to be confronted and dealt with, not because they were terrorists but on account of their hosting of terror. The arch-villain behind the existence of al-Qaida was a national of Saudi Arabia, a millionaire civil engineer, Osama bin Laden, who, it has been said, inherited $250 million at the very least. Taliban and bin Laden had a mutual dependence; they were two sides of the same coin. Bin Laden needed a safe haven and Taliban was strengthened by the terrorist's military and financial support. Both of them exploit the Afghanistan drug trade. The terrorist chief must be found and captured.

We have here a certain and rather intriguing link between religion and terrorism. It is worth examining in some detail. Taliban was headed by a number of mullahs, leaders of prayer with ministerial responsibilities. They emerged around 1992, after the retreat of Soviet forces coming to the rescue of a Communist administration had plunged Afghanistan into civil war. The mullah-ministers from the Taliban centre in the capital, Kabul, stated that Afghans had a 'rescuing religion' whose function was to rid Islam of poisonous Western influences. Afghans were to be purified by the all-knowing fundamentalists. There would be no doubts, no debate, no wide scholarship, no gambling, no music, and nothing much for women, denied any education and sunk in total inequality and subservience. A Ministry of Vice and Virtue was to keep morals on the straightest of paths and the Religious Police would deal with any dissidents. In this bizarre setting the Taliban regime kept control through exercising violence, although they could not in themselves be termed terrorist. There was every incentive for a ruthless international terrorist gang to feel welcome there.

THE MULLAH-MINISTERS FROM THE TALIBAN STATED THAT AFGHANS HAD A 'RESCUING RELIGION' WHOSE FUNCTION WAS TO RID ISLAM OF POISONOUS WESTERN INFLUENCES.

The story of al-Qaida is long and complex. It was in 1998 that bin Laden set it up, with the name 'the Base', as a service centre in Afghanistan for the many thousands of young Arabs who had come in earlier to help the Afghan resistance movement, the *mujahidin*, face Soviet troops in ten years of savage fighting. Although Afghans had received substantial US military aid and money from Saudi Arabia, bin Laden and his battle-hardened associates soon concluded that they must fight on all fronts, against Communism, capitalist countries such as the United States, their former backer, corrupt Arab regimes, and expansionist Israel. It was a potent, demonic mixture of an ultra-narrow religious creed, twisted politics, and a highly trained and well-armed adventurous band. Highly trained 'Afghan Veterans' began to show up wherever there was an Islamic struggle in Bosnia, Kosovo, Chechnya, Algeria, Somalia and Sudan.

> **IT WAS A POTENT, DEMONIC MIXTURE OF AN ULTRA-NARROW RELIGIOUS CREED, TWISTED POLITICS, AND A HIGHLY TRAINED AND WELL-ARMED ADVENTUROUS BAND.**

United States intervention in the Gulf War of 1991–92 put them into the front rank of bin Laden's enmity. They had sent 20,000 of their infidel troops to sacred cities in Saudi Arabia. American dollars had seduced Arab monarchs. It was vital to defend Islam against a 'Christian' crusade (even though the American advance was a rather materialist one). It was a Muslim duty to do away with those who sinned against the Muslim world and this would give Islamic religion and teaching extra power. It was necessary to take the battle right across to America.

On 12 October 1996, bin Laden declared a jihad against the United States and two years later put his name to a fatwa, a decree, to all Muslims to kill 'Americans and their civilian and military allies to be carried out in whichever country they are'. It was in an interview with *Time* magazine in 1999 that he made no secret of intensifying a wish to obtain non-conventional weapons: 'Acquiring weapons for the defense of Muslims is a religious duty. And if I seek to acquire these weapons, I am carrying out a duty. It would be a sin for Muslims not to try to possess the weapons that would prevent the infidels from inflicting harm on Muslims'.

IT WOULD BE A SIN FOR MUSLIMS NOT TO TRY TO POSSESS THE WEAPONS THAT WOULD PREVENT THE INFIDELS FROM INFLICTING HARM ON MUSLIMS'.

The United States, during these years, had a rather ambivalent relationship with the Taliban. There were rather inconclusive talks about possible pipeline facilities across Afghanistan for American and other oil companies tapping the great Caspian Sea oil reserves. In return for this and other concessions, Taliban was ready to sup with the devil and hope that nations other than Pakistan and Saudi Arabia would grant them state recognition.

With al-Qaida, of course, there could be no compromise. Agents of the CIA now and then despatched snatch squads to extricate bin Laden from his supposed cave bunker in the Hindu Kush mountains. President Clinton, in 1996, signed an Anti-Terrorism Act authorizing the freezing of terrorist assets. Every possible US device was used to search for and punish al-Qaida, for an attack on US soldiers in

Somalia in October 1993 which killed eighteen, in 1998 for their bombing of two US embassies in Kenya and Tanzania when 224 people died, and, once more, for an attack on the US warship, USS *Cole*, in Aden when seventeen of the crew perished. The despatch towards Kabul of seventy cruise missiles and a 5 million dollar reward for bin Laden's head did not achieve anything other than provoke bin Laden to issue a fatwa, placing upon all Muslims the duty of killing all Americans and their allies. Round-the-clock surveillance of Afghanistan was able to locate al-Qaida terrorist training camps for war veterans and fundamentalist converts, as well as arms stores and communication centres. Ultimatums went from Washington to the mullahs in Kabul, warning them that they would be held responsible for aggression against American citizens by terrorists in Afghanistan. These had little effect. Polite replies were despatched westwards saying that, of course, Islamic hospitality would never permit its 'guests' to be extradited.

When an aggrieved United States, in 2001, went to war against international terrorism and against the Taliban as hosts of terrorists, the debate raged internationally. Was a battle strike, hopefully pinpointing the whereabouts of a group of terrorists, the most effective way of countering an estimated 100 terrorist organizations, diverse in nature and motivation and locale? It was true that al-Qaida personnel were supposed to be at the core of many of these groups but the contexts in which they operated

WAS BOMBING THE RELIGIOUS TALIBAN THE BEST APPROACH TO 'TAKING OUT' THE TERRORISTS THEY HARBOURED?

were so different. Was bombing the religious Taliban the best approach to 'taking out' the terrorists they harboured? In sponsoring a coalition, military and political, against a Muslim country, was President George Bush calling for a contest with Islam in general? Many Muslim states like Iran, Saudi Arabia and Egypt were unhappy about this, believing that the people of the 'umman', the Islamic world community, should stand by Afghanistan, attacked in the name of a move against terrorism. There were Muslims in Indonesia, the Philippines and Malaysia who had to put up with sporadic terrorist activity at home and who now began to fear the prospect of US counter-action fanning out into South-East Asia as well as the Middle East.

The Taliban appeared broken and demoralized in December 2001 as their strongholds fell one by one. There was no evidence that the Afghan al-Qaida was in such a state as that and every reason to think that their global network of cells was undisturbed. Osama bin Laden lost no time in engaging in a propaganda war. While at first not admitting any responsibility for the 11 September bombing of New York and the Pentagon, he praised 'those youth who had destroyed America'. Newspapers, radio, videos, faxes and satellite telephones, and a pan-Arab satellite channel, al-Jazeera, located in the Gulf state of Qatar, were all used to beam his intentions across the world. Bin Laden would struggle relentlessly with three objectives in mind, namely, the removal of American forces from his native Saudi Arabia, the ceasing of sanctions against Saddam Hussein's Iraq, and a speedy resolution of the Israeli–Palestinian conflict. There was a clever lacing up of political and religious motives in this, with a reckoning that others in the Muslim world might forgive the terror methods that might have to be employed to realize these goals. For instance, while the Pakistan government (one of the three states recognizing Taliban) cosied up to Washington, there would be general support among the people for their Muslim brothers in Afghanistan. Bin Laden, sure of the Arab support that he would gain, ridiculed the thinking he saw behind Washington's name for the Afghanistan operation, that is, 'Enduring Justice'. Only the loyal followers of the Koran could bring justice to his fellow Muslims: it was never to be imposed from outside.

Bin Laden's al-Qaida remains a formidable world menace very much because it has tapped into the emotive springs of fundamental religious belief and linked them with other things that are fundamental in a different sense, that is, political imperatives that are coloured by hunger for power and hunger for food. A 'believing community' can easily become an unrestrained and violent force, not necessarily in general, but it may condone violence to achieve basic objectives. Al-Qaida is a well-organized and highly secretive terrorist network. Bin Laden's executive circle, the Shura, includes a dozen aides and representatives of the network in other lands, all experienced in mounting a jihad. There are a number of committees, for instance, a military one in charge of training, arms procurement, and terrorist strategies, a financial one whose resources are reportedly awash with vast proceeds from heroin and opium dealing, and a media one which has impressive technology and media competence. All these functionaries take an oath of eternal allegiance. It has been suggested that al-Qaida is not a hierarchical structure but a loose, rambling one, a 'spaghetti' type of organization. Whatever its nature, there is no doubt about its effectiveness. Apart from the military vanguard, al-Qaida draws strength from a web of commercial undertakings in various parts of the Middle East. There are companies trading in import–export, currency, chemicals and explosives. Roads and bridges and housing schemes are constructed by al-Qaida engineers. There are swathes of al-Qaida land, again in several countries, growing sesame, corn, peanuts and narcotic crops. This brand of international terrorism has a very substantial technological and commercial foundation.

THIS BRAND OF INTERNATIONAL TERRORISM HAS A VERY SUBSTANTIAL TECHNOLOGICAL AND COMMERCIAL FOUNDATION.

A coalition government for the rehabilitation of Afghanistan is now functioning in Kabul, watched by an American and British security force and perhaps eventually by international detachments. Will Osama bin Laden, the terrorist entrepreneur, be cornered in a cave? In past years he has slipped adroitly between Afghanistan, Pakistan and Sudan, with brief visits to Europe. If the leader were 'eliminated', would that really be the end of an extensive terrorist web? Would he not achieve immortality as a martyr? There is discussion, too, of the possibility of putting bin Laden himself on trial, whether in the United States or in an international court (which would not be able to impose a death penalty). In the case of a trial, lawyers would attempt to link directly the founder of al-Qaida with the planning and recent bombings in the United States and Europe. Cast-iron proof might be difficult to establish in a law court. There is almost certainly a great deal of 'classified' information about suspected al-Qaida involvement which has not yet been made public.

The peculiar links between international terrorism and the fundamentalist varieties of religion are likely to be around for a long time. There are many fanatics and martyrs, as the next chapter will show. And a chilling thought is that some fanatics may choose to threaten the world with biological or nuclear weapons.

chapter six

FANATICS AND MARTYRS

It is best to use the word 'fanatics' with some caution. Originally this word had a religious significance since it was linked to the word 'temple'. Now in everyday speech it is a word used to describe someone with excessive enthusiasm such as a football fan, a collector of antiques or a scientist hunting for rare plants. Many of the saints beatified by the Roman Catholic Church for centuries might be thought as fanatical in their inspiration and devotion. Another meaning of fanatic relates to attitudes and behaviour which may be difficult to tolerate because they seem so unconventional or unreasonable. The religious fundamentalists mentioned in the last chapter are frequently termed fanatics although this may lead to some confusion. Essentially, the religious fundamentalist is overtaken by an excess of regard for something like a particular belief or ritual or text such as the Bible or the Koran. This could be a commendable position but not so if they are unreasonable in never admitting anything other than their own opinions. They defend the narrowest of views, perhaps their whole way of life, with vehemence. Fanatics feel they have to act or interpret things in their own way. Most of them seek to defend their own beliefs and the absolute right-

MOST FANATICS SEEK TO DEFEND THEIR OWN BELIEFS AND THE ABSOLUTE RIGHTNESS OF THEIR CAUSE AT ALL COSTS.

ness of their cause at all costs. Such ingrained intolerance in religious or political beliefs, when they are unable to discern alternatives, can lead to lack of restraint and to the use of violence regardless of the consequences. That is when the religious fundamentalist and the political activist may be termed terrorist, although, of course, not all are so inclined, nor will terrorists readily call themselves fanatics, or fanatics admit to terrorism. A feature of some fanatics of the extreme variety and in some parts of the world is that they resort to suicide and martyrdom. This chapter will take a close look at this by considering at first fanaticism itself.

FANATICS IN THE MIDDLE EAST

Almost every day the press reports the latest suicide catastrophe. It is especially in the Middle East that fanaticism occurs. Examples of this are the organizations known as Hamas, Hizbullah and the Muslim Brotherhood, and the extreme wing of Jewish orthodoxy in Israel. Widespread fear and anxiety are certain, particularly among Israelis. The Hizbullah group has specialized in suicidal terrorism over the last twenty years. They have had several aims in mind. The Israeli security service is kept on a costly, time-intensive alert, Jewish settlements are being rendered unsafe by constant, explosive harassment. Palestinian sympathizers, however reluctant to endorse hit and run violence, are likely to revere a martyr, one of their 'liberators'.

Hizbullah is a fundamentalist and fanatical organization founded in Lebanon in 1982 as a militant wing of Shi'ite Muslims. Originally, this was a group feeling alienated and thwarted at home which then looked for a mission to consolidate its ranks. Foreign influences were to be expelled and a free Islamic republic created to replace a weak government. The message they eagerly adopted would get rid of infidels and defend both their religious and political beliefs. A mission, a jihad, would oblige dedicated followers to use all means to fight an enemy with the promise of Paradise as a reward. There are, however, differences between Hizbullah and other terrorist groups in the Middle East such as Hamas. In the first place, there is for Hizbullah the presence of a philosopher, Sheikh Muhammed Fadlallah, whose influence upon the movement has been considerable. A senior Shi'ite cleric, he has tempered the fanaticism of his nearest associates with something approaching modesty and moderation. Frequently, he has suggested that the group should think over its tactics and risks very carefully rather than give in to overhasty impulses. If you cannot persuade your enemies, then warfare is lawful from a religious point of view. Israel and its Western supporters in the United States are so powerful that there is no alternative than to try to match them with intelligence and fierce resolve. A powerful thrust at Israel's dominance should not be relaxed, he believes. Fadlallah's opinion of suicide as a last resort appears a little strange. The Koran forbids it, but for this sage the death of a believer is very likely anyway whether it is by one's own hand or the result of enemy action. Either way, suicide or death in battle are not tragedies, nor the consequences of despair. Death, in the right cause, is purposeful. Terror, if it is used, is 'Holy

EITHER WAY, SUICIDE OR DEATH IN BATTLE ARE NOT TRAGEDIES, NOR THE CONSEQUENCES OF DESPAIR. DEATH, IN THE RIGHT CAUSE, IS PURPOSEFUL.

Terror'. Nor are the Hizbullah, for this philosopher, in any way terrorists. They fight a Holy War for their people. A second difference from a group like Hamas, is that Hizbullah not only employs logic, but has social functions. It stands as the champion of better security for the poor and has set up a network of welfare centres and religious education centres. The logic and the moderation otherwise stand uneasily against Hizbullah's reputation for aircraft hijacking and hostage seizure, although these terrorism specialities have decreased in recent years.

An interesting last point about Hizbullah is the idea, prevalent in the West, that you never negotiate with terrorists. The *Guardian* reported on 17 November 2001 that the United States had secretly offered to forgive Hizbullah for attacks on Westerners in return for abandoning its struggle against Israel. This initiative from Washington asked Hizbullah to make a statement distinguishing between Islam and terrorism, or what was considered religious and legitimate on the one hand and criminality and terrorism on the other. Added to that, Hizbullah should withdraw from the Arab–Israeli struggle, give up its support for the *intifada*, and break links with other terrorist groups in Israel and Syria. Hizbullah refused to comply with these requests. The United States then countered with a freeze of Hizbullah assets. Undoubtedly, whatever the resolve and vigilance of Western governments, the terrorist potential of Hizbullah remains formidable.

Other groups have learned from the expertise of Hizbullah. In particular, Hamas, in the years after 1993, has used Lebanon to try out suicide techniques and to 'export' them to towns in Israel. After initial attacks on military targets proved difficult to sustain, Hamas moved towards the marketplace, the bus station

AFTER ATTACKS ON MILITARY TARGETS PROVED DIFFICULT TO SUSTAIN, HAMAS MOVED TOWARDS THE MARKETPLACE, THE BUS STATION AND THE ISOLATED SETTLEMENT OUTPOSTS.

and the isolated settlement outposts. Week by week civilians suffer greatly and the sense of security evaporates. Bombing was frequently the background to slow-moving peace nego- tiations, leading to Israeli accusations that Palestinians were not honest in their desire for settlement.

Hamas ('Zeal') was founded in the 1980s by fundamental Islamists in Gaza and the Occupied Territories of Israel, both places of poverty and seething unrest. Arabs there, without much in the way of weaponry, resorted to personal attacks, even suicide missions, as a means of demonstrating their anger in dramatic fashion. Iran and Saudi Arabia began to support them with funds and some crude elementary arma- ment and they found in Egypt radical friends who had been active since 1920. Fanatics, as the world terms them, are often able to articulate their wishes and demands. Within Hamas there has always been an energetic vanguard of young stone-throwers launching the protest of the *intifada* in Israel's streets and reaping a prominence in the world's media. In the backrooms of the Hamas movement there are journalists and Islamic scholars and aspiring politicians hammering out an insistent message of destruction to Israel. There is to be no manoeuvring with the enemy, no peace process such as is the weak defeatist policy by the Palestinian Liberation Organization. At least that was the situation before 1995; after that there was less fatalism and more realism. The PLO leader, Yassir Arafat, swallowed his distaste for no-holds- barred terrorism, and managed to convince the less extreme elements in Hamas that Palestinians needed to form a broad pacific front for talks with Israel and the West. There remains here a prospect of terrorism 'on hold'. On 25 January 2006,

Hamas unexpectedly secured a majority of votes in a general election. This now enables them to form a new Palestinian government. Will they not have to renounce their terrorism to be sure of outside Western funding for Palestinians? Certainly, Israel and the United States are unconvinced that the new shape of Hamas offers any alternative to their long-held objective of forcefully liberating Palestinians from oppressive Israeli occupation. Ministerial clothes appear not to disguise the resolute militant activist.

The Muslim Brotherhood was founded in Egypt in 1920 and has recently become much more active, spawning small like-minded groups such as Hamas and Al-Gama'a al-Islamiyy'a and a Jihad group (or Islamic Jihad). Terrorism seems endemic in Egypt. The Brotherhood takes its mission very seriously and, although it is the fighting wing which gets most attention in the media, there are vigorous cultural and social wings as well as Islamic indoctrination in the Sunni Muslim faith. Saudi Arabia and Iran financially support the Brotherhood. In many ways the Egyptians have to cope with economic and social insecurity, much of which the Brotherhood blames on a government they say is corrupt and religiously heretical. Terror methods involving bombs, guns and arson have been used against the police, judges, court officials, Christians, some business figures and foreign tourists. Assassination attempts have been made against President Mubarak and some of his minis-

TERROR METHODS INVOLVING BOMBS, GUNS AND ARSON HAVE BEEN USED AGAINST THE POLICE, JUDGES, COURT OFFICIALS, CHRISTIANS, SOME BUSINESS FIGURES AND FOREIGN TOURISTS.

ters. Although the Egyptian government might have some sympathy for the Brotherhood's call for the liberation of the Palestinians and for Pan-Arab unity, its counter-terrorism tactics have been severe. Many of the Brotherhood languish in prison, others have been tortured to reveal fellow conspirators. Lately, the Muslim Brotherhood has found it safer to take some of its initiatives further afield. They are suspected of a hand in the bombing of the World Trade Center in New York in 1994.

As the world knows, the fanaticism of the Arab can be matched by that of the ultra-nationalist, orthodox Jew. Many moderate Israelis deplore the descent of some of their fellow Jews into extreme violence towards Palestinians. One example of the fundamentalist position is that associated with Chicago-born Rabbi Meir Kahane, who arrived in Israel in 1971 with a message of hatred from believers. A group of vigilantes formed around Kahane, giving themselves the name Kath ('Truth'). With Kahane as something of a Messiah, they marshalled their resources to pour scorn on the attempts of the government in Tel Aviv, egged on as it was by Washington and London, to come to a fairer, lasting agreement with the Palestine Liberation Organization. Fortunately for Israel and for the Palestinians, the apocalyptic warnings of the Kath movement appealed to few and their extremism was generally cold-shouldered. Kahane himself was fatally wounded by an assassin, probably an Arab, in New York in November 1990.

FANATICS IN ASIA

Sri Lanka appals the world with its lasting experience of suicidal terrorism. The hit squad of the Tamil Tigers, known as Black Panthers, strap explosive devices to their waists. Every other Panther is a woman in her twenties who will go down to the target area appearing as if she were pregnant in order to conceal the explosive bundle. Since 1987 the Panthers have wormed their way into Colombo's government buildings, past the guards, to mark down a prominent politician or a general. Even a Tamil senator working to bring peace to Sri Lanka may become a victim of searing hatred and murder. In this way, the Panthers assassinated President Prendesa in 1993 and badly injured the present incumbent, President Kumaratunga, in December 1999. There is no return for the terrorist on this sort of mission. The cyanide capsule around the neck will be bitten and chewed to escape capture and interrogation. The Tamil Tigers are not primarily religious although some of their followers are Hindus. They are passionately sure they are right in fighting for a separate existence for the Tamils in the island, although they have already been awarded some autonomy. The extent of terror used is horrific.

THE TAMILS' MAXIM IS 'DESTROY EVERYTHING THAT DESTROY YOU'.

Their maxim is 'Destroy everything that destroys you'. For them there can be no other way. There is an extraordinary sense of group unity and personal commitment among these Tiger fighters who are very often teenagers. For such fanatics, death is an alternative to capture and imprisonment, rather as it was among Japanese soldiers during the Second World

War. In their sense of shared fate they compete for the honour of a glorious death.

Another country in Asia much troubled by fanatical terrorists is Japan. It was in 1987 that a crowd of young men began to gather around Shoko Asahara, a half-blind mystic who had made a living in Japan opening yoga and acupuncture centres and selling patent medicines. This group, calling themselves Aum Shinrikyo (the 'Supreme Truth') began by combining Buddhist and Hindu beliefs in a peaceful fashion, then they became increasingly preoccupied with Asahara's teaching, namely, that they must prepare themselves for some sort of cataclysmic happening which would precede a time of fortune and serenity. A Big Bang would be the prelude to heaven on earth. It has never been quite clear whether the Aum cult saw themselves as the victims or the agents of this dreadful happening. They appeared to have made the transition from waiting for Disaster to actually bringing it about. They had to be ready to face up to an enormous challenge with Asahara, the saviour, leading them into a new century. Disciples were recruited by the cult's 'missionaries' in Russia, Australia, Sri Lanka and the United States. More ominously, for a group ostensibly wedded to peace and fraternity, there commenced a frantic search for weapons, high explosives and guaranteed funds. Identifying the enemies of the cult as the evil representatives of the United States and capitalism in general, together with a search for sophisticated weaponry, was the sort of message that appealed to former members of the Soviet KGB and to discontented scientists and retired soldiers in Japan. Stocks of biological and chemical agents were built up. There was some rather unsuccessful casting around for any surplus uranium or weapons-grade plutonium.

The Aum Shinrikyo cult struck on the morning of 20 March 1995. The target was the crowded hub of Tokyo's underground railway. A dozen packages containing the nerve gas, sarin, were carefully placed in a number of subway stations. Soon, the stations were filled with dense clouds of gas which overcame the crowds leaving trains. Some 5,000 people were taken to hospital suffering from convulsions and respiratory problems. Twelve of them died. At first, it was not at all clear to the emergency and security services just what the cause of the incident was but investigations confirmed that the Aum cult had been responsible. Nine months went by before Asahara and a number of his close associates were pinned down and indicted for mass murder. This incident has aroused much alarm and not only in Japan. Was this outrage a foretaste of what terrorist fanatics might be able to do with chemical and biological weapons once they had mastered the problems of production and distribution? Prediction and prevention would be enormously difficult. These problems, the shape of terrorism in the future, are discussed again in Chapter 8.

WAS THIS OUTRAGE A FORETASTE OF WHAT TERRORIST FANATICS MIGHT BE ABLE TO DO WITH CHEMICAL AND BIOLOGICAL WEAPONS?

FANATICS IN EUROPE

Suicide squads have penetrated Europe. The Islamic Jihad group from Egypt found 'softer' targets in Croatia where a police station was bombed in October 1995, and in Pakistan where the Egyptian embassy became targeted by assailants. In both cases the terrorists were doing this in retaliation for the arrest of other Jihad members. Not one of the bombers survived the incidents. In Spain there is, too, the occasional self-inflicted death of someone carrying out a terrorist attack, although this may be accidental with the device going off when being carried or placed in position. In London, in 2005, as we have seen in Chapter 2, all four bombers resorted to suicide.

TERRORISTS AND SUICIDE

Suicide is a feature of terrorist behaviour among the Hamas and Hizbullah and Tamil Tigers. There is a great deal of speculation about this. There is some reason to think of three types of suicide, namely:

- those who are willing to murder others before they sacrifice themselves
- those who are prepared to kill themselves without harming others, for instance, those from the IRA who starved themselves to death in a Belfast jail in 1981
- those who undertake a high-risk mission, for example, an aircraft hijack, a car bombing, or a property attack, and are prepared to accept the lethal consequences of their action.

Every terrorist group allowing or even encouraging a member to commit suicide (with the promise of Paradise gained and honour among comrades) will then revere their hero.

WHAT SORT OF A PERSON IS THE VOLUNTEER FOR A SUICIDE MISSION?

What sort of a person is the volunteer for a suicide mission? Is he a 'loner', someone ostracized in the wider community, someone perhaps who shrugs shoulders at the prospect of a final ending? Chapter 4 has considered terrorists and their motives and warned against making deductions that were too simple. Yet the prospect of anyone facing the certainty of extinction after acting in a particular way fills most people with horror. If the terrorist shows no remorse towards anticipated victims is he mentally ill or temporarily 'off balance'? How far can we reconcile what appears to be temporary or permanent derangement with what so often turns out to be a capacity for logical and rational planning, calculation and preparation before the final incident?

Investigation of the New York bombing of 11 September has yielded some evidence of the mania and rationality of intending suicidal terrorists. Nineteen young men from Middle Eastern countries assembled at Logan Airport, Boston, that morning. Their preliminary planning in outline had been started months before, it seems, among members of a revolutionary cell in Hamburg. Final details were meticulously put together in Florida where some of the group had trained to fly jet aircraft. Tuesday was to be the day for the attack since there would be more business executives and government people on the chosen flights. There were to be no survivors from these extremely determined, clear-thinking young men. Transcripts from German Intelligence and from the FBI were able, during long-term surveillance, to home in on terrorist conversations on these lines:

'Make an oath to die ... Obey God ... stand fast'.

'Welcome death for the sake of God'.

'Remember to pray before reaching the target – then meet in Paradise'.

North America has only had to meet sporadic terrorism hitherto. Terrorists able to combine in thought, cold calculation and destructiveness and to go on to the 'nth' degree may well be able to do anything, anywhere. None of us is safe.

THE TERRORIST AS MARTYR

As we have already seen, the martyr is a common figure whenever terrorism breaks out and especially in the Middle Eastern countries and Sri Lanka. Any death of a terrorist is explained away as something expected and honoured. This is very much the feeling of the younger fanatic. Among older, more conservative leaders, for instance in Hamas and Hizbullah, there are signs of doubt about going all-out for death as an end to violence. **Deliberate martyrdom is ensured good media coverage.** Image and group identity are reinforced at the price, though, of lessening understanding by the West.

Europe also has had its martyrs. It was in the 1960s and 1970s, in what was then known as West Germany, that the Red Army Faction (or the Baader-Meinhof Gang) caused a great deal of alarm and havoc. It all began with student protest against authoritarianism and lack of reform in universities and fanned out into wider protests against the United States involvement in Vietnam and NATO. When student protestors became more forceful and violent, whipped up by alliance with other discontented factions, press and government called them German fanatics. A dedicated few engaged themselves in a relentless national and class struggle. Martyrdom was, for them, an end in itself, something that would renew the essence of their fight. The hunger strike was their main weapon. Nothing could be more effective in forcing a government to recognize that fanaticism was a lever for reform. At one point, in 1981, there were 120 hunger strikers in German jails, in a carefully organized symbolic gesture. Could the state allow them to die? Should they be fed by force and, if so, did this not violate their human rights, as they declared? Eventually, although several of the strikers died, most of them were talked out of their resolution. The collapse of the Berlin Wall in 1990 and the reunification of Germany were just two of the things that gave the earlier protestors other things to think about. Strong counter-terrorist measures soon reassured most Germans and by 1992 the fanatics were virtually disarmed, never to appear on the scene again.

NORTHERN IRELAND

Finally, there is the instance of martyrdom in Northern Ireland. For almost a hundred years, sacrifice has been a wholly understood if not expected end to contest. Until southern Ireland gained its independence in 1920, the Catholic Irish republicans fought fanatically against the occupying army of England. Neither imprisonment nor gun fighting diminished their fierce determination to be rid of the hated occupation. The death of an Irish rebel in Dublin Prison, in the streets or in the countryside, gave their comrades extra strength, buttressed their faith, and made sense of their desperate military actions. Defeat and imprisonment turned into victory through 'sacrificial martyrdom' and 'renewal through martyrdom'. This was the way to inspire and help recruit the next generation. Death is never defeat. Those

DEFEAT AND IMPRISONMENT TURNED INTO VICTORY THROUGH 'SACRIFICIAL MARTYRDOM' AND 'RENEWAL THROUGH MARTYRDOM'.

who had to suffer knew the truth about that and knew they were replaceable by others who would win in the end.

Michael Kearney, a Dublin professor of philosophy, has described what he terms 'the mythic logic of martyrdom' as a way of standing up to an oppressor Britain, and standing proudly, through 'sacrificial suffering'. This has brought Catholics on board more than any fusillade of shots or stone throwing. Even Christ had been a martyr in the eyes of Catholics in the ranks of the Irish Republican Army (IRA). In Kearney's view, 'hunger-strikes were better recruiters than bomb-strikes'. Certainly, the British government has learned during many years of 'terrorism' in Northern Ireland that a passive readiness to die for a cause is impossible to break with force.

The IRA soon realized the dramatic power of the hunger strike as had the Red Army Faction in West Germany. It has been said that hunger strikers in the notorious Long Kesh Prison in 1980–81 were driven along by politics but were inspired by myth. Like the terrorists in Germany, the Irish

THE IRISH PRISONERS DEMANDED TO BE TREATED AS PRISONERS OF WAR AND NOT AS COMMON CRIMINALS. prisoners demanded to be treated as prisoners of war and not as common criminals, but they were not prepared to accept the consequences of being tried by a military court as war criminals considered responsible for the indiscriminate murder of civilians. The British and German governments continued to regard them as political prisoners who were indicted for criminal offences. Probably in Irish martyrdom there is an element of nostalgia, harking back to the Dublin hunger strikes of 1920, a very real sacrificial memory. As for martyrs, they are 'keeping the faith', and that has both a religious and political meaning in Northern Ireland. What is beyond doubt now is that the starvation to death of Bobby Sands in his prison cell in 1983 brought about a vast amount of public discussion. The Whitehall government went on to open tentative talks with the IRA and with Sinn Fein, the political ally of the IRA, and with the Protestant Unionists, thus initiating what was to be termed, years later, the Northern Ireland peace process. In this part of the world, the fanatic and the martyr were at least closer to being understood, even though they would never be pardoned for their excesses.

chapter seven

TERRORIST METHODS

Terrorism has always been news, never more so than in the last thirty years. More than 8,000 incidents of international terrorism have occurred since 1968, according to a computerized database at St Andrews University in Scotland. This may not be an exhaustive record but it does point to the extent of serious incidents which have given rise to loss of life, extensive injuries, and much damage to property. This total works out at five incidents a day and at least two of these have involved death to innocent civilian bystanders.

This chapter will survey some of the methods used by terrorists and will instance a number of the most notable incidents between 1968 and 2005. Methods, such as those outlined, have not always been endorsed unanimously by certain terrorist groups, and this chapter will make some reference to today's anguished debate among Palestinians as to whether or not to continue their *intifada* campaign. There will also be a description of the dilemma facing the African National Congress fighters in South Africa only a few years ago, a dilemma which still faces those activists who know that only force counts, namely, do we use terror methods or do we not? State sponsorship is the next topic dealt with and this is a topic of considerable importance and anxiety in the contemporary world. Finally, there is a note about the financing of terrorism.

HIGHLIGHTS OF THIRTY-SIX YEARS OF TERRORISM

This list can only be a selection to give some idea of terrorism's frequency, nature and location:

- 1968   July – hijack of Rome-Tel Aviv plane by 3 Palestinians (the twelfth hijack that year). Trading passengers for Palestinians in Israeli jails. Negotiated solution.

- 1968   London – the Angry Brigade (young Londoners) let off 25 bombs, 1968–71.

- 1970   Jordan – August – Palestinians hijack 4 planes. One goes to Cairo, 3 are blown up on return to Jordan.

- 1971   Uruguay – Sir Geoffrey Jackson, British Ambassador, kidnapped by Tupamoros terrorists, held for 8 months.

- 1972   Munich – 8 Palestinian terrorists (Black September group) hold Israeli Olympic athletes hostage in exchange for 236 Palestinian prisoners. Gunfight kills 5 of the 8 terrorists and all 9 hostages.

- 1972   Lod Airport, Israel – Japanese terrorists (acting for Palestinians) use guns and grenades, kill 26, injure 80.

- 1973   Chile – September – President Salvador Allende assassinated.

- 1974   Paris – Japanese terrorists bomb discothèque, kill 2, injure 35.

- 1975   Vienna – OPEC (Organization of Petroleum Exporting Countries) summit meeting, ministers kidnapped, later released. German–Palestinian terrorists.

- 1977   Hans Martin Schleyer, German industrialist, kidnapped and killed by Red Army Faction.

- 1977   March – Rome – Aldo Moro, former Prime
           Minister, abducted by Red Brigade, killed
           after 2 months. (Reportedly, Red Brigade
           responsible for 14,591 attacks during
           1969–87.)

- 1977   Somalia – Lufthansa flight to Spain
           hijacked by German–Palestinian terrorists.
           German commandos kill 3 terrorists, cap-
           ture one.

- 1978   Ethiopia – attempt on life of Egyptian
           President Mubarak fails.

- 1979   Teheran – November – US embassy raided
           by Islamic students who hold 52 diplomats
           hostage for 444 days. Abortive rescue
           attempt ordered by President Jimmy
           Carter.

- 1979   Ireland – IRA kill Lord Mountbatten by
           bombing his fishing boat.

- 1980   Bologna – August – Italian right-wing
           group bomb railway station killing 84,
           injuring 180.

- 1980   Munich – September – German right-wing
           group bomb Oktoberfest celebrations,
           killing 14, injuring 215.

- 1981   Rome – May – attempt on life of Pope John
           Paul II by Turkish terrorist fails.

- 1982   London – July – IRA car bomb decimates
           troop of mounted Lifeguards.

- 1983   Beirut – April – US embassy. Islamic Jihad
           use suicide car bomb to kill 69.

- 1983   Beirut – October – US and French headquarters. Islamic Jihad use suicide car bomb, killing 299.

- 1983   London – December – IRA bomb Harrods store.

- 1984   Amritsar, India – Sikh terrorists seize Golden Temple. Indian security forces retake Temple. 100 people die.

- 1984   Lebanon – Terry Waite, Archbishop of Canterbury's envoy, abducted, held till 1992.

- 1984   Brighton – October – bomb attack fails to kill Prime Minister Thatcher at conference.

- 1984   London – December – IRA bomb discothèque.

- 1985   June – Rome to Cairo flight of TWA 847, hijack by Hizbullah, who want exchange of 776 prisoners. Aircraft moved to Beirut, Algiers, Beirut. Then, 39 American men held hostage in Beirut. Intense diplomacy and President Reagan yields.

- 1986   West Berlin – April – discothèque popular with GIs bombed by Libyan terrorists.

- 1986   Naples – June – Japanese terrorists bomb US Army club, killing 5, injuring 17.

- 1988   Lockerbie, Scotland – December – in-flight bombing of Pan Am 103 flight, probably by Libyans, killing 259 passengers, and 11 on the ground.

- 1989   Chad – August – in-flight bombing of French plane by Islamic Jihad, killing 171.

- 1991   Paris – Sharpur Bakhtiar, former Iranian Prime Minister, assassinated by Iranian terrorists.
- 1991   London – failed mortar attack on 10 Downing Street Cabinet meeting.
- 1993   New York – February – World Trade Center. Sunni terrorists attempt destruction with bomb and gas cloud. Partial failure but 10 killed, many injured. Suspects indicted eventually.
- 1993   Bombay – February – car bomb in retaliation for damage to Islamic shrine kills 400 and injures 1,000.
- 1993   Waco, Texas – April – forced suicide by members of Branch Davidian cult. FBI siege leads to 71 deaths.
- 1993   Somalia – October – car bomb at UN troop barracks kills 18. Al-Qaida suspected.
- 1994   Algeria – GIA (Groupe Islamique Armé) machine guns public places, killing 8, injuring 180.
- 1994   Jerusalem – Orthodox Jew enters mosque and shoots to kill 29, wounds 150.
- 1995   London – Canary Wharf business complex bombed by IRA, killing 2, injuring thousands.
- 1995   Tokyo – March – nerve gas attack on subway by Aum Shinrikyo cult, killing 12, injuring 5,000.
- 1995   Oklahoma City – April – federal building

bombed by Timothy McVeigh of Christian Patriots.

- 1995   United States – June – 'Unabomber' sends home-made bombs by post, killing 3, injuring 21. Found and arrested.

- 1995   Israel – November – Prime Minister Yitzhak Rabin assassinated by Orthodox Jew.

- 1996   Jerusalem – February – Hamas car bombs a bus, 22 die; Palestinians use car bomb to disrupt election, 22 die.

- 1996   Cairo – April – Gamat al-Islamija terrorists machine-gun, lob grenades, at foreign tourists killing 18.

- 1996   Lima, Peru – Japanese terrorists take all guests hostage at Japanese ambassador's reception. Negotiated end to this.

- 1996   Saudi Arabia – Saudi dissidents car-bomb US Air Force barracks, 19 die.

- 1997   Luxor, Egypt – November – Gamat al-Islamija terrorists kill 58 foreign tourists and 4 Egyptians.

- 1998   Nairobi and Dar es Salaam – August – US embassies car-bombed, allegedly by Al-Qaida, killing 224, injuring 5,000.

- 1998   Northern Ireland – despite the ceasefire, IRA terrorists bomb Omagh marketplace, killing 29 and injuring 250.

- 1998   Manchester – IRA attempt to wreck the centre of Manchester with car bombs.

- 2000   Yemen – October – USS *Cole* bombed,

probably by al-Qaida, killing 17, injuring 40.

- 2001 New York and Washington – September – 2 hijacked planes demolish World Trade Center towers; Pentagon is bombed; one other plane misses White House target. Worst ever disaster with nearly 3,000 dead.

- 2001 United States – September–October – United States and many other countries have anthrax spores sent to individuals by post. Some deaths in the USA.

- 2001 Jerusalem and Haifa – December – one car bomb in each, 25 killed.

- 2002 Island of Bali – October – car bombs in bar and discothèque kill 202, injure 209. Islamic suspects linked to al-Qaida arrested.

- 2003 Baghdad – UN Headquarters – August. Bombs kill 23, injure 100. At London's Heathrow Airport, 400 troops, tanks and 1,000 extra police. Deployed to foil possible plot to use surface-to-air missiles against aircraft.

- 2004 Madrid – bombing of trains by al-Qaida sympathizers, who are arrested. Kill 191, 1,900 injured.

- 2005 Thailand's first car bomb, in Sungai Kolch, kills 6, injures 40. London underground stations – bombing on 7 July, by 4 suicidal men whose motives are still controversial. Casualties are: 53 killed, 700 injured.

There is a follow-up attempt two weeks later, when the bomb devices fail to explode.

The above list of terrorist incidents reflects their prominence in the media. Over the last thirty years, the number of terrorist incidents in just Jerusalem and Haifa must run into many hundreds. No list could ever record the volume of continuous violence that scars society in Israel, Algeria, Sri Lanka, Colombia and, until recently, in Northern Ireland. The perpetrators of terrorism are 'media hungry' in their determination to shock the world. They are well aware that all of us spend a lot of time looking aghast at what has been called 'terrorvision'. An important point to remember about such a list is that it records the violent activity of a number of political groups as they hit the world's headlines, without labelling these groups as generally unacceptable or acceptable. Presumably these incidents strike most of us as cruel and intolerable but in some places a number of them will be regarded as legitimate expressions of a fight for freedom.

THE PERPETRATORS OF TERRORISM ARE 'MEDIA HUNGRY' IN THEIR DETERMINATION TO SHOCK THE WORLD.

THE USE OF TERRORIST METHODS: SOME EXAMPLES

Not only dates and places are highlighted in the above list. There is a remarkable variety of means of destruction and pinpointed targets. These are among some of the methods terrorists have used:

- arson, bombs and the threat of them, car bombs, chemical substances, hijacking, kidnapping and hostage taking, grenades, guns (small and automatic), knives and machetes, letter bombs, mortar and rocket launchers, stoning, suicide, vandalism

and these are some of the targets:

- aircraft, airports, banks, businesses, buses, diplomats, embassies, government personnel and offices, hotels, markets, military personnel and installations, religious figures and buildings, railways, roadways, shopping facilities, subways.

It is often pointed out these days by security services and terrorism experts that while the number of terrorist incidents and their frequency has been decreasing in recent years the number of casualties has grown quite markedly. The technology of terrorism has something to do with this. The use of remote controlled and delayed action devices and superior means of communication have made hit-and-run action a little easier and prompt detection and prevention rather more difficult. For those whose responsibility is security and counter-terrorism there will always be a problem with accurate prediction, despite the terrorists' use, now and then, of coded warnings. The impossibility of prevention is shown, most tragically of all, when terrorists strapped to a bomb blow themselves up or when a car bomb detonates.

The terrorist incident most difficult to anticipate is the one which leads to mass murder and widespread damage. The

USING JET AIRCRAFT AND ALL THEIR PASSENGERS AS SUICIDE BOMBERS HAD NEVER BEEN TRIED BEFORE 11 SEPTEMBER 2001. destruction of New York's International Trade Center on 11 September 2001 was a new method in that using jet aircraft and all their passengers as suicide bombers had never been tried before 11 September 2001. Unusually, too, no terrorists' organization revealed its identity or claimed responsibility for what they had done. A great deal of investigation had to be undertaken before the United States placed the blame squarely on al-Qaida. It seemed impossible to make out any understandable motive for doing something so destructive, indiscriminate and irrational. There were other grave terrorist worries in the autumn of 2001. Envelopes containing anthrax spores were sent to addresses in the United States and the resulting infection caused a dozen deaths. Subsequently, many countries in Europe had to deal with a spate of envelopes containing powder, fortunately harmless. It was to be expected that hoaxers would be ready to make a twisted contribution to anxieties.

TERRORIST METHODS IN DEBATE

In a chapter which outlines terrorist methods, it is interesting to consider occasions when terrorist groups have found they cannot unanimously agree to suggested methods. Often, a lively discussion has ensued and sometimes the organization has been in danger of collapse. Some methods will be abandoned, others modified to suit a particular political or ideological purpose. A terrorist scenario giving rise to much controversy is the *intifada* campaign of the Palestinians.

Box 4

A terrorist incident

Place

Munich Olympic Village, 5–6 September 1972

Incident

- Eight terrorists of the PLO Black September unit raid bedrooms of 9 sleeping Israeli athletes, in the early morning. They kill 2 athletes, hold 9 hostage.
- Terrorists offer to exchange hostages for 236 Palestinians held in Israeli prisons. Demand safe flight to an Arab country.
- Negotiations with Germany difficult. Terrorists threaten to kill one hostage every 2 hours if demands not met.
- Germany in evening offers 2 helicopters to take terrorists to nearby airbase for transit to Cairo for hostage exchange there.
- Terrorists taken to airbase then refuse further talks. Prearranged German rescue plan fails to prevent a shootout with terrorists hiding in helicopters and 3 of them die.
- Terrorists kill 9 hostages. Remaining 5 terrorists reject surrender plea.
- One terrorist late at night leaves a helicopter, destroying it with grenade. In further shoot-out 2 terrorists die.
- Ceasefire early next morning. Remaining 3 terrorists surrender and arrested. All 9 hostages, 5 terrorists, one German policeman, now dead.

Consequences

- Part-failure; part success.
- PLO fails in demand for prisoner release. Germans fail to resolve crisis.
- Success for PLO with world publicity coup (famous people, famous location).
- Germany and Israel straightaway form special counter-terrorist units.
- United Nations debates and committees begin work on specific counter-terrorist measures.

For fifteen years, since 1987, Palestinians have felt frustrated by Israeli occupation and rule in the West Bank and Gaza. They have orchestrated an *intifada* ('uprising' in Arabic), a series of demonstrations, with angry confrontations against Israel's security forces, strikes and riots. A civil disobedience movement has grown more and more violent. Stone throwing by unemployed youth has earned publicity but little sympathy elsewhere. The bullet and the car bomb were soon weapons in the hands of the PLO, Hamas and the Islamic Jihad. Once started, the progress of violence seemed unstoppable. Israeli counter-measures used heavy police and army presence, closures of schools, evictions, and punishment sorties on Arab land with tanks and helicopter gunships.

After four years or so of methods getting nowhere, the PLO resumed talking to the Israeli government. The more extreme elements in Hamas and the Islamic Jihad were now left with a straight choice: do we persist with the *intifada*, which can lay on the toughest of methods, vicious enough to alarm the world and force Israel to the negotiating table? As events have subsequently shown, these methods have not brought any positive, peaceful outcome. Predictably, the most violent methods only provoke a terrible counter-response. In December 2001 the confrontation between Arab and Jew in Israel was becoming catastrophic. Every day there was a fresh incident, usually that of a car bomb or suicide bomber decimating civilians and triggering the hardest of responses from a government feeling itself beleaguered. Together with a shoal of protests from a watching world there were appeals to both sides to show restraint and observe absolutely a binding ceasefire. Palestinians must lay aside their hopeless *intifada*.

For the Palestinian leader, Yassir Arafat, there was now no alternative. Terrorist methods would be no lever for a fairer land settlement and peace. He had, though, to reckon with three elements of the *intifada* and three sets of methods. There was the Tanzim front, a grassroots coming together of Palestinians who had faith in the democratic methods of spontaneous demonstrations and no patience with the idea that violence inflamed their opponents. They were the ones whose livelihoods had been shattered by the chaos of a divided community. Arafat thought he could reason with them about observing a winding down of aggression. The younger ones among them might be persuaded that their stones and Molotov cocktails were now ineffectual. There was the Hamas group, more fundamental Islamists, working out of sandbagged cellars and bunkers, whose objective was the complete liberation of their Arab territories and whose terrorist repertoire included everything destructive. Arafat sent out his policemen to arrest more than a hundred of these fanatics, worrying at the same time that this gesture might seem too feeble to Tel Aviv and far too drastic for most of his supporters. Then there was the Islamic Jihad (being blamed for the latest bloody incidents) who were on the rampage for the destruction of Israel and whose methods knew no bounds. Arafat was powerless here. Terrorist methods had had their day, as those in the 'outside' world could see, but how were these methods to be got rid of by those on the Palestinian 'inside'? As expected, Arab opinion ranges from 'extreme' to 'moderate'.

When are non-violent methods so unproductive that terrorists must replace them with 'action-tactics'? In the days of

THE HOPELESS PROGRESS OF THIS PROTEST FORCED THE ANC TO CHANGE ITS WAY OF OPERATING COMPLETELY. apartheid South Africa, the African National Congress (ANC) was the vanguard of a passive protest on the part of blacks. The hopeless progress of this protest in the face of a white government brutally screwing down all opposition forced the ANC ultimately to change its way of operating completely but this was only done after many days of debate. Nelson Mandela, in his autobiography, *A Long Walk to Freedom*, tells the story of how a revolutionary change in campaigning came about. Although this all happened over thirty years ago, Mandela's story does show how a terrorist group has to wrestle with the enormous problem of which methods to use.

To begin with, black protest was essentially non-violent, using non-cooperation with the authorities, and individual and mass defiance. The government would reply to this with a state of emergency, censorship of the press, forced eviction and confinement in 'special areas' and, increasingly, with tougher and tougher means of crowd control. It was in the 1960s that bullets replaced tear gas and water cannon and there were several mass killings of black people, in relentless crackdown. Were violent methods now the only way? Mandela describes the shift in thinking, which he and others reluctantly adopted, away from Gandhi's principle of non-violence-may-convert-your-enemy to a strategy of armed rebellion. State reaction was in itself violent: like had to meet like. There was much unhappiness about this. Surely, if the ANC preferred the gun then this

STATE REACTION WAS IN ITSELF VIOLENT: LIKE HAD TO MEET LIKE.

would expose innocent people to massacre by the white enemy? What sort of weaponry would be needed – guns, bombs, high explosives? It would be impossible to sustain a campaign using arms which were difficult to procure. Branding this as defeatist, Mandela and an emerging majority were confident that South Africa's black people would understand the need and the essence of such a change in strategy. New methods would constitute 'guided violence', a path of violence even though it was trodden in the dark.

Methods, then, were adapted to fall in with a changed sense of priorities, namely, to match the government on its own terms. Mandela, no soldier, as he admitted, was given the job of recruiting an army, to be called 'The Spear of the Nation'. He spent hours poring over the tactical advice of Fidel Castro, Che Guevara and Mao Tse-tung. Heading the list of possible terrorist methods was sabotage. That should not necessarily involve loss of innocent lives. It was cheap in manpower. Mandela set about working out selective forays against military installations, power plants and factories, and communication links. There would be some disabling of the economy but it ought to rock the government's complacency and steer them towards serious negotiation. If that did not work, then the ANC must be prepared to strike out with guerrilla warfare.

> **HEADING THE LIST OF POSSIBLE TERRORIST METHODS WAS SABOTAGE. THAT SHOULD NOT NECESSARILY INVOLVE LOSS OF INNOCENT LIVES.**

The sabotage campaign, compared with others, proceeded in fairly low key. Whatever the extent of its success there was immense political progress. Secret talks between the ANC and the South African government began in 1980. Ten years of negotiating trial and error finally brought into being a white-and-black administration, the Rainbow Nation. Apartheid had collapsed. And in 1994, the arch-terrorist (retired) became South Africa's first black President. The debate about methods is wider now. Had a resort to violence effected a seismic political change?

STATE SPONSORED TERRORISM

For at least fifty years, state sponsoring of terrorism has been a feature of the international scene. Seven countries are listed as active sponsors: Iran, Iraq, Libya, Lebanon, Syria, North Korea and Sudan. There is a two-way benefit in this sponsorship. Terrorist groups have practical support, financial aid, and the protection of a powerful guardian, and there is sanctuary in the event either of the success or failure of a mission. The patron state has advantages too. No state wishes to be revealed as aggressive and power-hungry, although there is always a readiness to oppose the foreign policies of others. Accommodating an active terrorist group may provide a host with just the cutting edge it needs to sustain its ideological thrust, as Iran, Cuba and Syria have found. Political initiatives leading to any form of modern warfare are expensive. Arranging for a small, keen, dedicated group to use violence as a means of realizing a political objective is a less risky and a cheaper way of adventure.

Libya is the best known of the sponsor states. Colonel Quaddafi has been an enthusiastic revolutionary for more than thirty years and one foremost in the terrorist export business. At home there have been ample funds, military personnel and hardware assigned to forwarding terrorism. When Quaddafi divided the world into 'imperialist lackeys' or 'freedom fighters' it was a straightforward task to deploy 'contacts' throughout Europe, Asia and South America and for them to coordinate terrorist strikes. Potential freedom fighters were welcomed to a Libya dotted with training camps and army bases. One estimate is that 8,000 or so recruits, some from eastern Europe but mostly Arabs, have gone onto terrorist courses in Libya. There they have drilled and had instruction in small arms, grenades, anti-aircraft guns and artillery, and anti-tank weapons. For many hours they have prac-

ONE ESTIMATE IS THAT 8,000 OR SO RECRUITS, SOME FROM EASTERN EUROPE BUT MOSTLY ARABS, HAVE GONE ONTO TERRORIST COURSES IN LIBYA.

tised on the ranges, and learned the reconnoitring and combat skills that special units like the SAS need. Laboratory instructors from Libya, Cuba and Lebanon coached would-be terrorists in the handling of Semtex plastic explosive and a variety of poisons and gases. The keenest recruits were shown how to hijack an aircraft or how to prepare for a suicide attack. Overseas, Libyan embassies functioned as safe havens for terrorists. They were able to provide intelligence about possible targets and supply false documents. Through the embassies, Libyan funds were channelled to ETA in Spain, to the Palestinians, to the IRA in Northern Ireland, and to the Sandinistas in Nicaragua.

Quaddafi's calculations were thwarted, first, by a US air strike in 1986 and then by the application of UN sanctions.

Quaddafi is now much more realistic. Libya can be safer and richer if terrorist export is allowed to die away and if diplomatic relations and trade is preferred.

Syria has been prominent as a terrorism exporter for at least thirty years. Its interests have been served by loud proclamations of support for Palestinian liberators and by equally loud hostility towards Israel. This clarion call has been popular at home and influential abroad. Any Middle Eastern state, like Saudi Arabia or Kuwait, sympathetic to US oil interests has feared attacks by Syria-backed fanatics. Possibly sixteen terrorist groups have found a warm Syrian welcome – Hamas, Hizbullah, the Palestine Liberation Front, the Popular Front for the Liberation of Palestine, the Islamic Jihad, and the Japanese Red Army and, almost certainly, al-Qaida. Like Libya there are extensive training schemes and all kinds of military and espionage equipment. Syrian television, radio and newspapers beam terrorist propaganda. There is a network of supply agents and transportation lines out to Lebanon, Iran and Yemen. Syria charges a fee to each recruit undergoing training in terrorist methods. Extra finance is reportedly raised through state-aided enterprises handling the sale of heroin and cocaine and also through a network of counterfeiting and money-laundering rings.

Iran, rather like Syria, has been an active state sponsor of terrorism for over twenty years and has also been regarded as a 'rogue state' offering facilities and shelter to such groups as Hizbullah, the more radical wings of the PLO, and Hamas.

There has been firm and generous support – ideologically, financially, militarily, operationally. The terrorist groups were regarded as puppets acting not only for their own ends against Israel and the United States but also buttressing the religious zeal and popular appeal of the religious clerics in Teheran. These were things the ayatollahs could never take for granted in a land as volatile as Iran. Teheran has been shrewd enough since the 1990s to make sure that its sponsorship is seen as more passive and conjectural than proved. Iranian nationals fighting alongside terrorist 'hit men' have posed as stateless 'volunteers' whose operations are carefully camouflaged. Certainly, since 1995, and again in common with Syria, approaches have been made to the politicians and economies of the West. Without disguising enmity towards Israel and backing for the Palestinian cause there have been closer contacts with Washington and London, despite anxieties as to Iranian interest in developing nuclear weaponry. An example of Iran (and Syria) 'coming out of the cold' is their collaboration with the United States coalition against al-Qaida in 2001. As one Washington senator remarked, 'it takes a terrorist to know and catch a terrorist'.

AS ONE WASHINGTON SENATOR REMARKED, 'IT TAKES A TERRORIST TO KNOW AND CATCH A TERRORIST'.

The sponsoring states have increasingly to face the dilemma of which side to favour, that of the terrorist bands or that of a more constructive linkage with the developed world. There is a need of brinkmanship here, with eyes on Washington and London, and there are already signs that state sponsorship of terrorists is decreasing in scale. Even some decency has been earned with Syria's unexpected acceptance as a non-permanent member of the UN Security Council. Syria and Libya are anxious to come on to the side of the angels; meanwhile, they remain on the US list of terrorism sponsors.

THE FINANCING OF TERRORISM

Since there is reason to believe that states like Libya, Syria, Iran and the others are withdrawing, however reluctantly, from terrorist sponsorship, then it must be that terrorists are having to rely more upon their well-wishers. This is true, above all, in the Middle East. It can never be easy to get the exact figure of terrorist funds for they must rely on complex links and subterfuge. No terrorist will stand up and turn out his pockets.

THE PLO'S ANNUAL INCOME MAY AMOUNT TO $600 MILLION.

Several estimates of terrorist wealth may not be too far off the mark. The PLO has been amassing capital ever since the mid-1980s. Each year, their income may amount to $600 million. The Palestinian Abu Nidal Organization (closely linked with Libya, Iraq and Syria) has lately moved out of terrorist sorties into big business and shady financial dealing and there the assets may be of the order of $400 million. Aum Shinrikyo, the terrorist syndicate, is thought to treble that figure. Hizbullah is not finding an annual income of perhaps $100 million at all dependable though it may vary with the blow-hot, blow-cold nature of political confrontation in Israel. Hamas, the fiercest terrorists of them all but with a tight network of subscribers, relies on something like $70 million each year. Yet external funding may be in doubt, should they not renounce their terrorist methods, as we have noted earlier. In contrast, ETA and the IRA, though receiving monies from abroad, have been carrying out terrorism on a shoestring.

Most wealthy of terrorists, Osama bin Laden, is seen by the US State Department as a Midas figure. A personal fortune of, perhaps, $300 million has gone into tremendous investments – in banking, airport construction, farming, diamond dealing, and the opium trade. Funding from this store must go into al-Qaida coffers in possibly thirty countries. As the actual head of the business side of terrorism, it will not be too easy for bin Laden to operate it from a remote cave-complex in Afghanistan.

The financing of terrorism is to be discussed in the final chapter, Chapter 10, as one aspect of an urgent international effort under way to track down and put an end to it. A final point here is that investigation of any financing going towards terrorism is enormously problematic.

INVESTIGATION OF ANY FINANCING GOING TOWARDS TERRORISM IS ENORMOUSLY PROBLEMATIC.

It is difficult to distinguish legitimate and illicit transactions, many of which are put under covert wrappers or else handed over without a 'paper trail'. Donations to cultural and social projects and to educational foundations may seem transparently honest but part of this may be siphoned off into rather doubtful channels. Terrorist funding may accrue out of bank robberies, money laundering, counterfeiting, hostage ransoms, protection rackets and narcotics handling. In numerous Arab countries and in

South-East Asia, monies may come in from émigré groups in Europe and the United States, from well-wishers who would be appalled if they knew that their gifts were diverted into violent activities. Terrorist methods in themselves are mostly inexpensive: it is the support of terrorist groups which demands finance. This is a point which is never lost on those who have to plan counter-terrorism.

chapter eight

FUTURE TYPES
OF TERRORISM

The prospect of world war has almost vanished with the end of the Cold War. Apart from the regional hostilities which are with us still, there is a different threat to world peace in the shape of terrorist groups in widely separated places attempting to deliver political and religious messages in highly dramatic terms. In their single-mindedness and despair they may be tempted to use methods which lead to injury and destruction on a cataclysmic scale. This is a different scenario from past types of terrorism when specific objectives were thought about, targets were identified and marked down, operations were planned and executed and, generally, deaths and injuries were not of massive proportions.

If the horrific events of 11 September 2001 did not, in fact, change the world, they certainly changed what many Americans call the 'risk-picture'. The terrorists responsible for toppling the World Trade Center had no compunction in killing some 3,000 people; they went to great lengths to plan things, to learn how to fly aircraft, and how to set up the operation with fiendish resolve. We all must now face a risk-picture where there is a **WE ALL MUST NOW FACE A RISK-PICTURE WHERE THERE IS A POSSIBILITY OF SUCH A HIGHLY ORGANIZED, MAMMOTH TERROR EVENT OCCURRING AGAIN.** possibility of such a highly organized, mammoth terror event occurring again. What happened was an instance of Mass Destruction Terrorism, sometimes referred to as Non-Conventional Terrorism. After 11 September everything is possible where terrorists may threaten or actually engineer the use of biological agents, chemical substances, or nuclear devices and use them on a scale sufficient to lead to widespread injury and damage. This chapter will discuss in turn each of these destructive capabilities and will end with a note about ecoterrorism and cyberterrorism.

BIOTERRORISM

Something was known about the feasibility and effectiveness of biological terror weapons already in the 1930s when the British government began to take seriously reports of experiments being carried out in laboratories in Nazi Germany. The First World War had seen the employment of poison gases by Imperial Germany and it was thought possible that Hitler, himself part-gassed in Flanders trenches in 1916, might consider using gases or other noxious devices as a terror weapon in desperate wartime circumstances. Britain did follow up this idea by undertaking an ambitious series of experiments and field trials at its defence laboratories at Porton Down. US military establishments were working on similar, sometimes collaborative lines. The work was highly secret and all facilities were elaborately guarded to prevent any access by the unauthorized. The Cold War years of the 1950s and 1960s led to a spurt in research. British and American military scientists carried out clandestine tests from the air and on the ground, studying the dispersal and possible effects of non-lethal sprays simulating anthrax and smallpox and of a plague bacterium which resists multiple drugs.

THE COLD WAR YEARS OF THE 1950S AND 1960S LED TO A SPURT IN RESEARCH.

It is only in very recent years that much has become known about the government research into the possibilities of biological warfare. The publicity about this and revelations that Britain had actually test-infected a Scottish island have led to continuing controversy. True, these methods had not been used in the Second World War but should a democratic state ever be looking into the possibility of deliberate spreading of disease like bubonic plague or anthrax as an agent of mass destruction? (This was an addition to the debate about aerial bombing.) In regard to possible terrorist use by an individual or a group, Porton Down has concluded that the risk is

SHOULD A DEMOCRATIC STATE EVER BE LOOKING INTO THE POSSIBILITY OF DELIBERATE SPREADING OF DISEASE AS AN AGENT OF MASS DESTRUCTION?

not great, given that there are so many obstacles to overcome, first, in producing biological agents of suitable quality, then to ensure that there are enough of them to make up a lethal dosage, then to arrange for appropriate and safe storage and, last, to make sure that a means of delivery is the right one and an effective one. Technically, if all these barriers can be crossed and the agent is sufficiently refined to be prime and potent, then it can be considered 'weapons-grade'. Difficulties such as these help explain why few terrorist groups have sought to acquire biological agents and even fewer have tried them out. Bioterrorist incidents have happened, as when the Japanese Aum Shinrikyo cult diffused sarin nerve gas into the Tokyo underground system in 1995, or in October 2001 when the United States was convulsed by an anthrax scare. Then there is real fear and disruption but the actual effects of the terrorist weapons have been fairly short-term. This is not to say that worse may not happen somewhere and sometime.

THE ANTHRAX SCARE OF 2001

The worst seemed to have happened in Florida in October 2001. On 5 October, Robert Stevens, a Florida journalist, died from inhaling anthrax. Detectives were able to isolate traces of the anthrax on the man's computer keyboard. Within the next few days there were reports that a similar 'potent' strain had been found in letters sent to Senator Tom Daschle, on Capitol Hill, and to Tom Brocaw, a well-known television presenter at NBC News, also in Washington, and to the Governor of New York State. Other spores were found in letter bins in government buildings. Prompt investigation found that a number of letters being received in New York and in Washington were containing white or brown powder. There was no smell and the powder could be lethal. If it were spores of anthrax, then the infection could be via the skin, that is, cutaneous anthrax, or it could be breathed in as inhalation anthrax. Was this terrorism at the price of a postage stamp? Apart from threats to prominent public figures, could this be an attempt to disable the United States through mass infection and its consequence of panic? Government research was to be given total priority. President George Bush put the entire nation on a state of high alert.

WAS THIS TERRORISM AT THE PRICE OF A POSTAGE STAMP?

It was soon established that many envelopes were being posted from addresses routed through Trenton, New Jersey. Most of these envelopes, after scientific analysis, actually held samples of quite harmless powder. On the other hand, and a reason for some concern, there was conjecture about whether the anthrax samples that had tested positive were sufficiently 'weaponized' as to present a major threat of widespread and very serious infection.

ONE EFFECT, IF NOT THE INTENTION, OF BIOTERRORISM, IS TO PUT INTO THE PUBLIC MIND A SILENT THREAT, THE IDEA THAT NOBODY CAN KNOW IF THEY ARE SAFE UNTIL IT IS TOO LATE.

Much harm had been done already, since one effect, if not the intention, of bioterrorism, is to put into the public mind a silent threat, the idea that nobody can know if they are safe until it is too late. The only thing Federal authorities could do to allay public confusion was to arrange screening of the public and extensive searching of letterboxes and sorting offices. Again, the tests largely proved negative although the anthrax infection had claimed four lives and hospitalized at least a dozen people, some of whom were postal workers. Large supplies of anti-anthrax drugs were sent to pharmacies and health clinics.

Who could be responsible for this terrorism? What motives might there be for sending suspicious letters not only to important people but also to anti-abortion clinics and Jewish groups? Did this point to what might be termed 'domestic' terrorism rather than an international one? What was the possible origin for those samples that were actually anthrax spores?

President Bush was quick to declare his belief that Osama bin Laden and al-Qaida were likely to be responsible both for 11 September and for the anthrax attack. There had been warnings from intelligence agencies of the possibility of a second rash of major terrorist attacks upon the United States either by al-Qaida or another fanatical Islamic group. Once more, it might be a suicidal attack. There were numerous reports in the American and European press of mysterious go-betweens negotiating purchase of biological agents out of eastern Europe to be consigned for use by al-Qaida. Despite much media interest and comment, these leads proved non-conclusive.

Could Iraq be the culprit? Saddam Hussein, after all, had had no hesitation in 1988 in using mass destruction weaponry against the Kurdish minority in the north of his country. Baghdad was thought to have started a biological warfare pro-gramme after the Gulf War in 1991 and to have accumulated appreciable stocks of missiles containing biological and chemical toxins. Again, an interesting lead ran into the ground when statements from the FBI and the CIA stressed that there was no firm evidence that a foreign government or laboratory was involved. Nor was it likely that Iraq or any other state had perfected an anthrax weapon.

Then, most dreadful of thoughts, might the anthrax have originated in the United States? In mid-October, it was the *Washington Post* that printed a belief from Washington offi-cials saying there was evidence suggesting a domestic origin. First tests revealed that the strains from Florida and New York, at least, closely resembled a strain developed by earlier military research in the United States, known as the Ames Strain. It was not impossible that samples of this quite viru-lent strain had been acquired by individuals, possibly through research stocks in university laboratories or pharmaceutical companies, and then perhaps passed on or stolen by others who had a criminal and hostile purpose in mind. The Oklahoma bombing had shown how ruthless extremist groups or a lone terrorist could be if they could get hold of a very real potential for public disruption (see Chapter 4). It was possible that a right-wing group or even Americans sympathetic to Islamic fanatics could have been instigators. Yet, for the domestic terrorist, there are many difficulties to surmount, as we pointed out earlier – difficulties of production, quality control, storage and dispersal, difficulties which might be thought of as deterring all but the most obsessive and competent of terrorists.

The anthrax scare in October 2001 led to much anxiety internationally. Envelopes with powder turned up in more than twenty other countries including Kenya, Brazil, Japan, Pakistan, France, Morocco, Lebanon, Lithuania, Portugal, Hong Kong, Slovakia and Australia. Surprisingly, Britain, a staunch ally of the United States, was not one of the recipients.

SURPRISINGLY, BRITAIN, A STAUNCH ALLY OF THE UNITED STATES, WAS NOT ONE OF THE RECIPIENTS.

Almost all these findings were declared to be a hoax, although hospitals were having to accept suspected cases of infection.

The result of all this does not paint a happy picture. There are people out there who are anti-life and anti-social and who are prepared both to endanger health and to induce widespread public fear. The hoaxer, and there must be many of them, is clearly a low-level terrorist who is difficult to catch. His motives seem irrational. The result is a major upset to society's daily life. What it does not necessarily lead to is public panic even though the press on both sides of the Atlantic printed PANIC in large letters in headlines. A responsible, restrained and objective press, even if fewer newspapers are sold, can be an effective means of counter-terrorism. Rumours need to be scotched. The anthrax incident clearly demonstrates that bioterrorism is a psychological weapon with the potential of causing mass hysteria and feeding conspiracy theories.

CHEMICAL TERRORISM

The anthrax scare understandably resulted in an avalanche of media comment and some not at all helpful exaggeration and speculation. There was, however, a reasonable amount of authoritative advice from government sources where a fine balance needed to be struck. Giving too much information about a range of possible dangers spreads wholesale alarm. Too little information results in complacency and lack of vigilance. As for counter-terrorist measures no government wants to risk supplying those tempted to terrorism with up-to-date facts about antidotes and preparedness. Government contingency plans were in hand to deal with the actual and potential means of bioterrorism in late 2001. What might happen in the case of chemical terrorism was an unknown factor and too much theorizing about it increases public alarm.

From time to time newspapers and television have carried carefully presented discussions of the possible use of chemical weapons. Porton Down scientists have stressed the difficulties that chemical and biological terrorists face. Both have technical problems in production where particles need to be fine-milled, neither too small nor too large, to prevent effective dispersal. No terrorist can forecast the weather at the time of operation. This and other factors can affect the state of the substance when it is being moved or stored safely. The terrorist has somehow to forecast and calculate the right time for the substance to be in a dependable and usable state. Whereas explosives can be kept under wraps, as it were, for just the right moment for impact, chemical substances may deteriorate and be rendered unstable by delay or mishandling.

To resort to chemical terrorism you need ideally to have a degree in chemistry, otherwise, it is not advisable to make a chemical weapon your first choice.

TO RESORT TO CHEMICAL TERRORISM YOU NEED IDEALLY TO HAVE A DEGREE IN CHEMISTRY, OTHERWISE, IT IS NOT ADVISABLE TO MAKE A CHEMICAL WEAPON YOUR FIRST CHOICE.

Scientific discussion suggests that two types of chemical terrorism pose significant threats. In the case of mass destruction attacks, toxic substances may be released into town centres, farmland, water supplies, and crowded places such as supermarkets and railway stations. In a sense this sort of terror is as old as the history of poisoning the enemy's wells and food supplies. Fortunately, there have been very few instances of such tactics succeeding in modern times. The other type is much more common when, for example, there is a deliberate attempt to blackmail the producer and supplier of a particular food product or something that is alleged to have been tested on animals. A chemical substance may be introduced into what is regarded as an offensive product. A number of foodstuffs and drinks have been polluted in this way in

Britain and the United States, resulting not so much in human injury as in the public refusing to buy the product and a consequent economic loss. Possibly, those responsible for this sort of terrorism, which might more properly be described as criminal vandalism, are people with a strong sense of indignation and filled with an ethical move to set things right.

Compared with the biological terrorist the chemical terrorist can operate with less scientific knowledge and competence. Many of the ingredients are easy and cheap to buy and one or two additives, carefully mixed, may add to the effectiveness of what turns out to be a menace. The terrorist's stock can be prepared and moved around fairly conveniently to avoid detection. The means of dispersal can be relatively cheap and not too difficult to arrange. Only prompt security alertness prevented the Aum cult in Japan from spraying hydrogen cyanide in central Tokyo in 1995. The underground system of Tokyo has now been fitted with sensors to detect chemical diffusion. Elsewhere, in the United States, the FBI has revealed that the al-Qaida group were trying to buy crop-spraying aircraft possibly with a chemical attack in mind. Once more, we have to reckon with the possibility that there is never any warning until the strike has taken effect. Again, this is a terror weapon with obvious psychological potential. On a larger scale, there is every sign that a number of states possess considerable stocks of chemical weapons, though, of course, they may be deterred from using them, reckoning that that would invite reprisals as well

THE FBI HAS REVEALED THAT THE al-QAIDA GROUP WERE TRYING TO BUY CROP-SPRAYING AIRCRAFT POSSIBLY WITH A CHEMICAL ATTACK IN MIND.

as condemnation. Iran, North Korea, Russia, and perhaps one or two eastern European countries are known to have these stocks.

International action by way of counter-terrorism is now urgent and essential. The UN General Assembly in 1972 in consultation with the World Health Organization drew up a Convention on the Prohibition of Chemical and Biological Weapons which, so far, 154 member states have signed. This agreement was to take further the attempts by states way back in 1922 to frame a Geneva convention to outlaw biological forms of warfare, although terrorism in that shape by others than states was not envisaged. The Convention of 1972 laid down strict rules about prohibition of certain substances and methods, listed mandatory measures of control, and provided for the preparedness of counter-action by governments and medical authorities. This action does not now seem watertight, for twenty or so of the signatories admitted that they did have stocks of biological weapons and, indeed, half of them had proof-trials in hand. There was a good chance that these governments were researching the practicability of missile delivery and going further to enquire into the usefulness of radiological emission, herbicides and defoliants. Equally, there was every possibility that terrorists might gain access to experimental sites and the actual things being tested. President George Bush and others are now insisting on improving precautions against the possibility of terrorists' illicit threats and action. Tighter legislation and surveillance are to plug loopholes (see Chapter 10 for UN action in this field, dating from 1997). Ideally, existing stocks of toxic weapons and production plants should be got rid of within ten years. All involved in handling toxic substances, when they are studied, used in research, modified in trials, and shipped, must be bound by the strongest of ethical codes and inspection procedures. Any suspicious outbreak of leakage of information must be investigated immediately by expert teams. All states must allow free access to 'challenge inspections' at twelve hours' notice. A response to mass destruction terrorism on these lines sounds fine and may go some way to reassure the public that their protection is a priority. The Convention rules that all states are to guarantee unrestricted access to surveillance. Again, this is a constructive provision until one remembers that three years of enquiry by twenty-three United Nations never settled the truth about Saddam Hussein's weapons stocks and the extent to which these fed into terrorist hands.

THREE YEARS OF ENQUIRY BY TWENTY-THREE UNITED NATIONS NEVER SETTLED THE TRUTH ABOUT SADDAM HUSSEIN'S WEAPONS STOCKS AND THE EXTENT TO WHICH THESE FED INTO TERRORIST HANDS.

Even so, in some quarters, there lurks the suspicion that certain governments like those of the United States and the United Kingdom will continue Porton Down types of research, justifying this as a defensive measure 'in the public interest'. It is well known that official quarters are apt to defend their stocking and use of lethal agents and to explain their accessibility by declaring that these substances have a 'dual-purpose' use, that is, they have a weapons potential and they can also be used in legitimate industrial processes.

NUCLEAR TERRORISM

This form of mass destruction terrorism represents the 'end of the line' in most imaginations. The nuclear devastation of Hiroshima and Nagasaki in 1945 demonstrated the awesome power of nuclear weapons. Over the last half century, at least fifty states have developed a nuclear arsenal. More states than that have developed civil uses of nuclear fission. The proliferation from Non-Nuclear Weapon States to Nuclear Weapon States is a problem that the Non-Proliferation Treaty of 1968 attempted to tackle. In good faith, 180 states sought to build a system that would restrain rather than inhibit the spread of nuclear armaments among states and, most importantly, to prevent rogue access to military nuclear capability. Additionally, there would be rigorous controls put in place to prevent illegal trading in fissile materials and deter any secretive work to enrich uranium from weapons grade to reactor grade, and there would be moves to make all nuclear plants absolutely safe from radiation seepage and sabotage.

The United Nations gave the task of controlling proliferation to the International Atomic Energy Authority (IAEA), which had been set up in Vienna in 1957. Their responsibility was twofold, to encourage countries to develop nuclear power for peaceful and industrial purposes, and to put in place and maintain safeguards against harmful application of nuclear energy. One hundred states agreed to a carefully organized control system which was to put teeth into the treaty provisions. More recently, the IAEA has established an Emergency Response Centre to react to radiological emergencies following a terrorist attack.

Nuclear terrorism could use two particular methods:

- the use of a nuclear device to bring about mass murder and extensive destruction
- the threat, or the actual use, of radioactive materials in an attack on a nuclear power plant or similar installation. This radioactivity could be delivered using conventional explosives to force entry and disperse the hazardous material.

Incidents typical of the first method will hardly ever happen since no terrorist organization is likely ever to have the finance or the technical knowledge necessary to process uranium or plutonium to produce a bomb, and to operate the device. Even so, we should not disregard the fact that there is plenty of advice about the making and assembly of nuclear devices on the internet and in public libraries. It is not impossible that a 'dirty bomb', an unsophisticated radiological weapon, could be assembled for use, perhaps, as a large car bomb. The

IT IS NOT IMPOSSIBLE THAT A 'DIRTY BOMB', AN UNSOPHISTICATED RADIOLOGICAL WEAPON, COULD BE ASSEMBLED FOR USE, PERHAPS, AS A LARGE CAR BOMB.

second method faces us with quite a different risk, namely, that a terrorist group would not need nuclear weapons, as such. Brandishing conventional weapons, and having reconnoitred carefully, a group could carry out a determined assault on a nuclear reactor which would result in irreparable damage to the reactor, the plant, and the surrounding environment. Whether or not there was a threat issued beforehand, terrorists would achieve front-page publicity and, if security were lax, would cause maximum damage at relatively little cost to themselves. The possibility of this happening to any of the hundreds of nuclear reactors in the world would be a sort of nuclear blackmail, something almost impossible to anticipate and, should it ever happen, an incident which would be most difficult to control. The disasters, some years ago, at Three Mile Island and at Chernobyl both illustrated the effects of 'melt-down' and raised questions about management and security.

Mass destruction using hijacked aircraft and attempts at biological and chemical terrorism have brought the prospect of mass destruction through nuclear terrorism very much into contemporary debate. There is an obvious black market in fissionable material such as enriched uranium and plutonium in parts of the former Soviet Union where there are consistent reports of thefts from former nuclear sites. Certain other countries, such as Libya, Iraq and Iran, as we have noted, have the capacity and probably the willingness to trade radioactive materials and information about nuclear processing and, since international monitoring and inspection have been refused, it is not clear how far their nuclear programmes have been developed. So much radioactive material is in transit these days all over the world that it might not be too difficult to hold up a convoy and steal its precious load. Also, there is something of a 'brain drain' of nuclear scientists and technicians, certainly from Russia and possibly Czechoslovakia, who

THERE IS SOMETHING OF A 'BRAIN DRAIN' OF NUCLEAR SCIENTISTS AND TECHNICIANS, CERTAINLY FROM RUSSIA AND POSSIBLY CZECHOSLOVAKIA, WHO MAY BE INDUCED TO PART WITH VALUABLE INFORMATION.

may be induced to part with valuable information. In the United States, intelligence sources have been quoted recently as thinking that the millionaire terrorist, Osama bin Laden, is active in the marketplace for radioactive materials and that he is wealthy enough to offer inducements to retired or unemployed nuclear scientists. Of course, this procurement would be only the beginning of any nuclear terrorism since its development needs large-scale processing plant. This may be only a rumour but the ominous fact remains that, given the absolute death-wish impulses witnessed in 2001, we cannot rule out the chance of a holocaust being brought about through mass destruction terrorism.

ECOTERRORISM AND CYBERTERRORISM

These are two types of terrorism which have developed rapidly in recent years and are likely to give us food for thought in the future. In the eyes of the law, incidents of this type are indictable as criminal but from a moral point of view and, given that these may result in injury and considerable dislocation and damage, they can be termed terrorism.

Ecoterrorism is something that has appeared on the fringe of the environmentalist or 'green' movement mainly in the developed world. A small minority hold such strong feelings about environmental exploitation and pollution that they are ready to push their case violently. Already, we have seen instances of protestors destroying fields growing genetically modified crops, sabotaging crop-spraying machinery, attacking logging camps, destroying dams and electrical installations. Research establishments thought to be involved in vivisection or other animal experiments are burned down and their employees threatened and harassed. Maximum publicity is the clear objective of such activity.

Cyberterrorism in the computer age is an attack on information systems rather than on people. Its consequences can be devastating. A so-called 'hacker', usually a lone individual sitting at a computer keyboard, has power, inventiveness and secrecy to cause immense, sometimes irretrievable, harm to institutions and other people. Using a variety of electronic devices, such as a 'virus' or a 'worm', the hacker may access confidential records, telephone and media sources, financial and commercial data, governmental and scientific projects. More clearly a form of terrorism, an individual bent on destruction may be able to access and interfere with air traffic and ground transport control systems.

AN INDIVIDUAL BENT ON DESTRUCTION MAY BE ABLE TO ACCESS AND INTERFERE WITH AIR TRAFFIC AND GROUND TRANSPORT CONTROL SYSTEMS.

Obviously, there is a grave danger of major dislocation and personal injury. As with ecoterrorism there is little warning of what may ensue.

DISARMING TERRORISM

It is not the intention of this chapter or of the book as a whole to spread alarm and distress about what the future may bring. To build public awareness means that reliable information and calm assurance about contingency plans must be readily available. If we are realistic in weighing up the possibility of various dangers, and calm about it, we are well prepared. A larger consideration, one that the United Nations constantly urges and something we can all support, is the reduction of world stocks of deadly weaponry and the curbing of nuclear proliferation. Progress there will make for a safer and better world – one in which terrorism fails to breed and flourish.

chapter nine

COUNTER-TERRORISM:

the piecemeal approach

Counter-terrorism has to do with the prevention and control of terrorism. In most countries there have been shifts in its purposes and methods and, generally, countries have dealt with isolated incidents or sustained campaigns in an independent, piecemeal fashion. They have done their best to recognize motives and to look for those thought responsible in an ad hoc attempt to tidy up after it has happened. Sometimes, as a result of painstaking police investigation or a rigorous army sweep, people are arrested, tried, imprisoned, even extradited. More often, the counter-action has been, as it were, to douse the flames but not put out the fire. Northern Ireland's 'troubles' are a sad example of that. Not everything, though, has been unilateral and left to lone chance. From time to time the United States has required its security agencies, the FBI and the CIA, to work in liaison with similar groups in Canada, Central America or Europe. In Britain, MI5 and Interpol have acted in harmony. Obvious questions take up much government time. Why did it happen? Who is responsible? Might it happen again? How do we protect ourselves and prevent it?

Put candidly, the counter-terrorism scene has been a morass of principles, dimly perceived, strenuously argued and variously interpreted. Meanwhile, terrorism is a world growth industry. Universally now, it is said, terrorism requires a global response in counter-action. Readers of this book will have noticed the constant refrain that while terrorism is a global phenomenon indeed, its character and extent and methods are so diverse that each outbreak of violence needs separate consideration and treatment. This does not preclude international homing in on the problem, rather, it calls for it.

COUNTER-TERRORISM, TO BE EFFECTIVE, DEMANDS THE CLOSEST CONSULTATION ABOUT PRINCIPLES AND WAYS OF WORKING.

Counter-terrorism, to be effective, demands the closest consultation about principles and ways of working. Strategies and programmes of prevention and control will greatly benefit from being devised at international level, for implementation at national, possibly regional, level. We need a 'workshop' approach.

This chapter will outline what is being done about counter-terrorism, as we say, in a piecemeal fashion, as individual governments such as Britain and the United States wrestle with its problems. Is terrorism crime or is it war? Are there moral issues at stake which entangle the actions proposed? What can the law do to protect the community and deter and prevent attacks upon it? In conclusion, Chapter 10 will take a broad look at today's efforts to bring states together in common decision and action.

COUNTER-TERRORISM IN THEORY: ETHICAL ISSUES

Would a government have any credibility or respect if it did not act promptly and clearly to deal with terror incidents? That no state can do anything else than 'take on' its ideological, political, religious 'challengers' is a crude rule-of-thumb precept, doggedly held for centuries, which unhelpfully blunts numerous keen questions. How much call for change and peaceful protest is allowable without repression? (Without permitted moves for change, would any society ever have progressed?) At what point does protest become unallowable – if there is incitement to violence and recourse to it? Regimes which are authoritarian appear to have less trouble with moral issues and harsh control methods than democratic states. It is the latter that frequently worry about whether their proposed control methods lead to injustice or violate the basic freedoms of a civilized society. All too often, the anguish is presented to a government on a plate by a league of other protestors, morally insistent ones.

The difficulty is that both sides bring moral issues into play to justify or condemn counter-terrorism approaches. A state has a stern constitutional charge to protect its people against subversion and sabotage. Fine, in principle, except that, on occasion, protestors will dispute every move of a state's counter-response; holding firm to their own beliefs and preferences, they will condemn what is said and done by authority and, in desperation and anger, use increasingly violent tactics. Basically, that is the chain of consequences underlying the actions of the IRA, of ETA, and of the Latin American terrorist groups and of the *intifada*. Terrorists see themselves as victims of a repressive, hypocritical regime

Terrorists see themselves as victims of a repressive, hypocritical regime which cannot even understand their case.

which cannot even understand their case. Then, they must fight. Moral issues have an element of calculation. The terrorist estimates the fragility, the patience and the sensitivity-to-public-criticism of the state enemy. The fighters of the IRA would reckon that one more terror thrust by the IRA would, of course, cause moral outrage in the

British mainland but bring Whitehall a little nearer to tentative negotiation. And it worked. In those instances, Britain, like any other democratic state with a counter-terrorism policy, had also to judge just the amount of force to exert to break terrorism, without leading to a gross miscarriage of human rights. The possibility of innocent casualties in a response sortie, while regrettable, could be justified morally if the Greater Good prevailed. Unfortunately, as with Bloody Sunday in Ulster, and with the de Menezes shooting in London in July 2005, human judgements can be tragically hasty and imperfect. Ultimately, again for the democratic community, it is to the law they look for sustaining moral principles and for getting counter-methods 'right'. Are most legal systems, with their moral armoury and with long laid-down codes of indictment and punishment, really best equipped to deal with the diversity of terrorism? Supposing that there are simmering grievances of all kinds, even hatreds, at the root of so much terrorism, are the conventional processes of the law, as we know them, the appropriate ones for making what will usually turn out to be political judgements? The difficulties for the rational statesman are only just beginning. They walk a minefield. For many of their constituents the clamour will rise: 'never mind the justifications, where's the action?' For many liberals, this recipe has been seen 'as chilling as it is counter-productive'.

ARE MOST LEGAL SYSTEMS REALLY BEST EQUIPPED TO DEAL WITH THE DIVERSITY OF TERRORISM?

COUNTER-TERRORISM IN THEORY: BRITAIN AND THE LAW

Each state's piecemeal approach results in piecemeal law, despite the best intentions of a government to be all-inclusive. For a start, how is terrorism to be defined? Not at all easily, as we saw in the first chapter. At this point, we can illustrate something of the problems with a legal approach by outlining the recent legislation that two states are putting into place, namely, Britain and the United States.

Britain has Acts of Parliament specially designed to deal with terrorism, the Prevention of Terrorism Act of 1999 (superseding one of twenty years earlier) and the Anti-Terrorism, Crime and Security Act of 2001. In each case, the British government has drawn up a set of protective and preventive measures. The main provisions in the law of 1999 could be listed as follows:

- the Act defines terrorism thus – 'the use or threat, for the purpose of advancing a political, religious or ideological cause, of action which involves serious violence against any person or property, endangers the life of any person or creates a serious risk to the health or safety of the public or any section of the public'
- the Act represents a comprehensive protective device for the public, improving on the patchy and temporary legislation then in practice
- the Act serves as a code under which terrorists may be charged and arrested
- the Act puts an end to summary exclusions and extradi-

tion procedures. Each case will be carefully examined with a right of appeal. (This part of the Act was framed with the injustices meted out to IRA terrorists in mind)

- police methods such as stop-and-search must be confirmed by the Home Secretary
- certain organizations thought to be menacing to public safety, for instance, those who incite violence, are to be proscribed, with a right of appeal to an independent body.

This legislation is designed to take account of threats by those residing or travelling within Britain and by anyone foreign to the country.

'Alarming!' 'Far too harsh and draconian!' These were among the milder epithets coined by the Labour government's own members in 1999. The Conservative opposition was more charitable, making the point that the Act was a much-needed instrument but acceptable 'only if the shackles on our liberty are removed'. The Home Secretary's assurance that there was 'a world of difference between an individual's right to freedom of expression and protest and the plotting of serious violence' was knocked around a good deal in the press. How would the degree of 'serious violence' be assessed and who would be there to do that? Where else than in Britain could you be sentenced to ten years in jail for speaking at a meeting? The speaker had the anti-apartheid movement in mind where many in Britain had strongly supported the fighters of the

WHERE ELSE THAN IN BRITAIN COULD YOU BE SENTENCED TO TEN YEARS IN JAIL FOR SPEAKING AT A MEETING?

African National Congress. How possible was it always to understand what 'incitement' meant? What would be the position of those seen taking part in an organized demonstration or a 'sit in' which was blocking traffic? Suspects would see their basic rights eroded. If this Act were interpreted too enthusiastically by the police, might it not clamp down on Speakers' Corner rights to free speech and association?

On 14 December 2001 a new counter-terrorism Bill received royal assent in London. The Anti-Terrorism, Crime and Security Act 2001 was to be a comprehensive attempt to plug loopholes and create a rigorous system of protection and deterrence. Significantly, there is now an association between anti-terrorism and crime, in that criminal law is to be amended and extended to defeat international terrorism. The Act's fourteen sections and twenty-seven schedules are highly detailed but the chief provisions are these:

- 'terrorist cash' and property are to be seized and forfeited (on a magistrate's order)
- suspect financial transactions are to be frozen
- suspected terrorists or members of a suspect group are to be certified as a preliminary to detention or deportation. There is a right of appeal
- incitement to racial or religious hatred will be a penal offence. Guidelines will be published
- biological agents (viruses, bacteria) are never to be transferable without authorization
- nuclear weapons are never to be exploded, acquired, developed, purchased or sold by individuals

- nuclear sites and transport of fissile materials are to be stringently controlled for security
- airfields, air transport and aircraft are to be accorded the strictest security
- police powers are to be regularized, for instance, in regard to stop-search-and-arrest, search warrants, fingerprinting, examination of persons and vehicles, permission for lawful assemblies and demonstrations, and the photographing of suspects
- 'communications data' may be scanned and held 'for the purpose of safeguarding national security'. The 'providers' of these communication channels will be asked to volunteer to keep records of their clients' use of channels. All this is to be in the interests of safeguarding national security, and the prevention and detection of crime
- hoaxes involving noxious substances will incur severe penalties
- information about acts of terrorism must be divulged: non-disclosure is an offence.

European Union anti-terrorism procedures are to be observed by Britain to do with extradition, the freezing of assets, and liaison with joint investigation teams and counter-terrorism programmes (see Chapter 10).

The provisions have been given in some detail since they are innovative in many respects, and the consequences of that have raised many loud cries. Britain's Defence Secretary, Geoff Hoon, told the House of Commons that we could not build a Fortress Britain and so we had 'to manage the risks'. The new system would be a fast-track approach without mass roundups, Britain was so obviously a prime target. This was a public emergency. His remarks had something in common with those from Washington when he added (in much lower key) that we had not only to undermine international

BRITAIN'S DEFENCE SECRETARY TOLD THE HOUSE OF COMMONS THAT WE COULD NOT BUILD A FORTRESS BRITAIN AND SO WE HAD 'TO MANAGE THE RISKS'.

terrorism but we had to try to understand it. That would require 'integrated political, economic, legal and military actions'.

Through November 2001 the Bill passed through the House of Commons though not without being roughly pushed from side to side. The House of Lords, as the upper chamber, was determined to give these counter-terrorism proposals a minute scrutiny. They inflicted seven defeats on the Government's Bill. 'It's Orwellian', one peer declared. 'Rammed through by a huge Labour majority', was another view. Liberals on all sides raised questions about official interference with citizens' human rights. They wondered whether the steamroller approach was not built on assumptions, some prejudice, and a good deal of political expediency. With 200 pieces of legislation on the statute book and a fourth terrorism Bill in five years, did we really need another Bill – from a government in panic? The Lords saw the conventional presumption of innocence before any conviction of guilt as being in danger. Could it be that as long as guilt was presumed there would then be no overall need to prove it? They shared unhappiness, 'a creeping sense of worry', at the prospect of the authorities trawling through confidential e-mails and internet browsing. Would medical and revenue documents become prey to official 'fishing expeditions'? If disclosure, under some form of penalty, was the order of the day, who would ever be the one to decide whether the material was at all related to 'national security' (that very vaguest of terms) or if there were grounds for 'reasonable suspicion of terrorist activity', as the Bill put it? It was in the House of Lords that peers questioned Whitehall's attitude to asylum seekers (a topic fiercely debated up and down the land). Would not Nelson Mandela, if he had fled to Britain in the early 1960s, have been sent back to his 'terrorist' compatriots in South Africa? It could not be right to see a terrorist behind every tree and to detain him indefinitely. It must never be the case that a convicted terrorist was extradited from Britain to the United States where a death penalty ruled unless (in accordance with European Union law) there was an assurance that no execution would follow. It was the Lords who threw out (their term) the possibility of indefinite detention, without full legal representation. They insisted that internet and e-mail providers be required to sign a voluntary code about keeping client records. Nor could they tolerate an edict against what was said to be racial or religious 'hatred' without very clear guidelines. Otherwise, it was said, Salman Rushdie might have been jailed.

Government Bills brought before Parliament, as we have seen, are battered almost beyond recognition. The general picture has become quite intense throughout 2004 and 2005.

Many in the House of Commons and in the House of Lords are worried about two parallel threats to freedom, namely, that of extended powers of control and investigation by security forces and then the tabling of tougher legislative proposals in Parliament. Controls, for instance, appear sterner, pre-emptive and heavy-handed, limiting freedom of movement and association. Are these not likely to alienate communities from which resentful and violent youth doubtless emerge? Powers to close places of worship, to ban 'extremist' groups, and ever greater possibilities of stop-and-search are especially controversial. Second, an Act designed to enhance 'protection of the community' is still exciting strong criticism from a lobby of liberal parliamentarians and lawyers. This is the Prevention of Terrorism Act 2005. Proposals most found fault with appear to be these:

- powers to enable arrest before committing an incident, that is, 'an act preparatory to terrorism'
- a charge of 'indirect incitement to commit a terrorist act'
- a charge of condoning, 'justifying' or 'glorifying' terrorism
- powers to deport an individual on grounds of fomenting terrorism
- internment for a period without specific charges or trial (at first, the government wanted a 90-day maximum period then compromised at 28-days' limit).

The power to make control orders is central to this Act. By official order, certain obligations are to be imposed upon 'individuals involved in terrorism-related activity' for the purpose of preventing further involvement in such activity. Obligations are manifold in prohibiting or restricting the possession of specified articles or substances, communication with specified persons or associations, movement within Britain or from it. Passports may have to be surrendered and access to particular places permitted. A suspect may be searched and photographed, his movements monitored electronically. In the widest sense, it is ordained, terrorism-related activity has to do with the preparation, instigation and commission of nefarious acts and with conduct which facilitates that behaviour where such conduct is held to give 'encouragement, support and assistance to would-be terrorists'. In effect, the Secretary of State may make a control order against an individual if there are 'reasonable grounds' for suspicion and if such action protects the public.

Certain provisions in this act have led almost to uproar among a range of leading civil society organizations. It is felt strongly that in the context of an ill-advised and counter-productive 'war on terror' (so-called) legislative means such as these pave the way for an equally misguided 'war on Islamic extremism'. Is not this simplistic and inflammatory stance likely, they say, to further offend and marginalize important sections of the community we are supposed to protect? Again, it is asked, in what ways will the authorities indict any individual for the new offence of 'indirect incitement'? Such persons are to be refused asylum, excluded from entry to Britain. Some will be deported. An international database of suspected individuals 'whose activities or views pose a threat to Britain's security' is to be compiled. Altogether, there is a long and loud controversy, publicly aired, as to the government's right and capacity to discriminate, charge, and then imprison those whose 'values' and 'opinions' are considered to challenge the ones we hold as British and sacrosanct. How free, it is asked, is the freedom legislators are setting out to protect?

COUNTER-TERRORISM IN THEORY: UNITED STATES AND THE LAW

President Bush, after the September outrage, spoke of his country as 'at war' with terrorism and promised legislation to fight something going far beyond conventional criminality. In his view anyone who in any way finances, harbours or defends terrorists is himself a terrorist, in other words, there is no distinction between terrorists and their friends and sup-porters. Meanwhile, in Britain the government had been at pains to bring a raft of legislation forward to tighten up pro-cedures against terrorism, without explicitly using the word 'war'. Something similar in intention to the British anti-terrorism legislation was hastily constructed by the US Administration towards the end of December 2001. Known widely as an Act Uniting and Strengthening America, the new Act, the USA Patriot Act, would supersede earlier legis-lation from President Clinton's time in 1996. Introduced as a Bill in October 2001, it was cleverly framed as an Act for 'Uniting and Strengthening America by Providing Appropriate Tools Required to Intercept and Obstruct Terrorism' – the PATRIOT Act (stressing the first letter in each word of the title). There were many provisions for enhancing domestic security and curbing international ter-rorist attacks. New investigative procedures would allow the FBI and other federal security bodies to put wiretaps on to suspects, and permit unspecified and undefined interception of website browsing and e-mail activities, again, by suspects, all this without involving the opinion and authorization of a judge. Search warrants could be issued and searches carried out without prior warning to anyone. Any group 'seeking to influence the

ANY GROUP 'SEEKING TO INFLUENCE THE POLICY OF A GOVERNMENT BY INTIMIDATION OR COERCION' WOULD BE LIABLE TO PROSCRIPTION.

policy of a government by intimidation or coercion' would be liable to proscription. There would be a prompt and most thorough clamping down on money laundering or any suspected deviation of funding towards terrorism. The House of Representatives passed these provisions through by an overwhelming majority though not without an appreciable amount of political gamesmanship and lobbying by civil rights groups. In the Senate it was different and the debate proceeded at a snail's pace, to the deep concern of the White House. There were impassioned complaints from Senators aghast at 'closing down our open society' and 'at the snooping appetites which trump privacy'. It was absolutely vital to protect the United States against terror attacks – this was war. Was the price of counter-terrorism, however, that of compromising our civil liberties? Would life become so transparent that we must not mind who wanted to know our confidences? In most respects, both in the United States and in Britain, it was the upper house of parliament and the pressure from lobbyists that delayed the implementation of counter-terrorism measures. Ethical and legal issues have been prominently to the fore, as most people have been relieved to see. These were regarded as putting the brakes on a state's right to commandeer private and personal information on the merest suspicion of a criminal offence which might be quite unrelated to terrorism. A measure of the US government's concern about protest about the new Act was that the Senate updated the Act's provisions in July 2005 and in December 2005, to moderate a number of the requirements that liberal quarters found objectionable.

Ultimately, the administrations got their legislation through after many torrid sessions. Much governmental impatience, if not fury, was evident at the protracted delays in upper houses. David Blunkett, Britain's Home Secretary, accused the Lords of deliberate sabotage. He roared (rather extravagantly) that the naive had shown their fangs. It was time to stop 'this silliness'. Huge and essential parts of the Bill were being 'kneecapped'. In the United States, Attorney-General John Ashcroft, introducing a new Department of Justice anti-terrorist bill in December 2003, had similarly lashed an all-night Senate sitting. 'Your tactics', he said, 'only aid terrorists; [they] give ammunition to America's enemies and pause to America's friends.' The American Civil Liberties Union, throughout 2003, maintained a rigorous campaign to offset Ashcroft's proposals which they considered 'fundamentally alter the Constitutional protections that allow us to be safe and free'. Nevertheless, compromise by both governments was in the air. Counter-terrorist moves remained tough but the rights of the rest of the community were now more plainly respected. Investigation and disclosure were now repackaged to allow for prior notification and judicial review. A stern watch is still being kept

INVESTIGATION AND DISCLOSURE WERE NOW REPACKAGED TO ALLOW FOR PRIOR NOTIFICATION AND JUDICIAL REVIEW.

on what happens among congressmen and senators. Legislation (and legislators) must be 'combed through'. The government has attempted to meet unhappy critics with a programme entitled 'Are We Safer in the Dark?' where the public must be taken (with care) into its confidence over possible threats and practicable measures. A 'Sunshine Week – Your Right to Know' will have the purpose of enlightening and reassuring. After all, it is pointed out, Homeland Security is a mutual responsibility.

Clearly apparent in today's United States (as in Britain) is what may be termed a 'watching brief' working carefully in two domains, that of federal law and that of the federal intelligence services. Legally, the provisions of the Patriot Act of 2001 are being continually reappraised and updated. Effective counter-terrorism through law sets out to enhance border security, the surveillance of immigration and emigration, together with wider jurisdiction over bomb threats and incidents. Governmental concern is to improve the collection and sharing of information between the intelligence community and state lawyers. An illustration of this is the 'roll-on' concept of renewing year by year the National Emergency proclaimed after 9/11 when a state in crisis may authorize prompt and strict law enforcement. Thus, for instance, Acts such as the Public Health Security and Bioterrorism Preparedness and Response Act (2002), the Air Transportation Safety and System Stabilization Act (2001), the Terrorist Bombings Convention Implementation Act (2002) are all the time on the front of desks in Washington. It must be Never Again!

COUNTER-TERRORISM IN PRACTICE

What is proposed and augmented in practice must, of course, be undergirded by legislative statutes. Understandably, both in Britain and in the United States, political questions and reservations keep on reverberating as measures deemed appropriate and legal are put into effect. The issues of 'appropriateness' and 'legality' are raised all the time and are sounded more emphatically as measures are reviewed and legal standpoints reassessed. Rosalyn Higgins, an eminent international lawyer, points to the absence of an agreed definition of terrorism as a hindrance to counter-terrorism practice. If terrorism is so varied and so case-specific it will be almost impossible to get the firm legal grounding that will make most counter-action legitimate and publicly acceptable. All too obviously, for Higgins, the term 'terrorism' has no legal significance. It is not an umbrella concept. Rather, it is a form of shorthand referring to a number of problems with shared elements and which are strongly condemned by civilized societies. There is certainly the stuff of debate here about a 'term of convenience', as this lawyer puts it.

HOW FAR CAN WE BE SURE, FACE TO FACE WITH TERRORISTS, THAT WHAT IS BEING DONE IS APPROPRIATE AND JUST?

Above all, if we agree with Rosalyn Higgins, how far can we be sure, face to face with terrorists, that what is being done is appropriate and just? Could there be a risk that heavy-handed over-reaction at a time of crisis and public alarm bears down indiscriminately upon the liberties and livelihoods of the entire community? (This complaint was often urged violently in Northern Ireland, apartheid South Africa, among Palestinians, and in parts of Latin America.)

Some of the flurries of controversy about anti-terrorist law and practice in Britain have been noted earlier. Meanwhile, in Washington, the US Department of Defense met head-on flurries of legal and ethical protest and justified this by declaring that it was urgent to put 'new capabilities' into force. A National Security Agency (NSA) would be given wide investigative powers. Their counter-terrorism practice had these priorities:

- the overall objective of counter-terrorism is 'spoiling action, deterrence, and response'
- 'spoiling' or weakening a terrorist organization depends upon accurate information about their strength, equipment, skills, logistical capabilities, customary tactics, a profile of leadership, source of supplies, and links with other individuals and groups
- levels of terrorist threat to the United States must be appraised – critical, high, medium, low, negligible, and appropriate response planned
- action by security teams and agencies must be tightly coordinated, carefully programmed, and be legitimate.

Further practical approaches to counter-terrorism being tried out at the moment in the United States and in Britain (in liaison) are these:

- enquiry into the reported aims of specified terrorist organizations
- recruiting and training special police/military units to pre-empt and prevent threatened attacks if intelligence services report these

- increased physical security and checks in 'sensitive zones' for personnel, buildings, and daily procedures
- use of intrusive surveillance technology where practicable, again in vulnerable areas
- searches, inspection of computer traffic and office files may be necessary in time of peril subject to legal advice and permission
- a reserve policy of 'irregular' police work using 'informers' or infiltrating undercover agents
- a range of sanctions and punishments to be in hand for anyone indicted for terrorism, e.g. stop-and-search, charge-and-arrest, trial (criminal court or special tribunal), internment, extradition, even capital punishment (the latter not in Europe)
- a policy of no ransom to hostage-takers, no concessions through negotiations with terrorists
- a move against any state involved in terrorism by means of diplomatic and economic boycotts, the freezing of assets and trade, the seizure and inspection of suspicious documents, scrutiny and control of air and sea linkages, possible military action
- the reserving of opportunities for mediation, 'open channels' for the option of basic dialogue with the possibility that terrorism may be restrained.

Altogether, the thinking behind these approaches is to raise the costs of terrorist action and to remove its benefits. (It should be noted, in regard to mediation and dialogue, that while governments understandably take the hardest of lines in public, there have been times, usually when hostages are being held, that secret parleying takes place.)

RENDITION

A new word appears in the newspaper columns, 'Rendition'. Readers, and, possibly, some sub-editors will have been thumbing dictionaries. Rendition, or 'extraordinary rendition', is defined authoritatively as the flying of terrorist suspects to third countries for interrogation. A number of things have led to liberal unease and protest. First, suspects may be sent to countries with poor human rights records where even torture may be practised. Second, it is believed that the American CIA has set up a network of secret prisons in Europe where 'renditionees' may be held awaiting further transfer. Next, it seems as though several hundred aircraft may have been chartered by the CIA shuttling covertly in and out of British and other European airports. This possibility appears strengthened by the wall of silence that meets enquirers who then naturally suspect tacit connivance in an inadmissible programme. Denied representation by lawyers and the International Red Cross, families have no means of knowing where related suspects are being held or transported. Finally, there is a sour note in the whole enterprise where security sources, on being repeatedly approached, admit to 'erroneous rendition', a pompous and clumsy way of saying that a suspect, grabbed off the street, later turns out to be innocent. Lately, the United States Secretary of State, Condoleezza Rice, has perhaps rather lamely stated that her nation would never consign suspects to a flight to torture. In any case, 'rendition takes terrorists out of action and saves lives'. (For many, such an assertion begs a number of awkward questions.)

In Britain, law lords have denounced in ringing terms any possibility of turning a blind eye to the consequences of 'rendering' terrorist suspects. US senators have also given voice to dissatisfaction over the operation. In both countries there is evidence that lawyers will not rubber stamp what they consider to be inhuman provision. They evidently fear that with another turn of the screw we should find ourselves shorn of those civil liberties we are fighting terrorists to defend.

chapter ten

TERRORISM:

international efforts to
defeat it

The last chapter dealt with the counter-terrorism efforts of individual states, in what was termed a piecemeal approach. This chapter, the concluding one, will be concerned, fairly briefly, with the enormous international efforts now being mounted to work against terrorism. The efforts described are these: that of the United Nations (UN), that of the European Union (EU), and that of the United States – all as a sequel to the horrendous terror attack of 11 September 2001.

THE UN SYSTEM AND COUNTER-TERRORISM

Three fields of activity will be outlined here: the counter-terrorism efforts of the UN's specialized agencies, the treaties now in force to give strength to UN efforts, and the concerted work to put an end to the financing of terrorism. These are all huge operations.

In the UN, member states, meeting in both the Security Council and the General Assembly, have called for intensified international action and cooperation. The UN is never just a talking shop. The General Assembly is a forum with power to devise treaties, acts and Conventions; the Security Council of 15 members is the executive arm of the Organization. The 185 member states are obliged to observe Conventions and Resolutions after they have been voted into effect. The General Assembly is now developing new international legal instruments, in addition to 12 anti-terrorist treaties already in operation.

The UN is also a system of organizations, specialized agencies, and programmes, collectively referred to as the UN system, and these have played a key role for many years in international efforts to defeat terrorism. Actions these specialized organizations have taken following 11 September are these:

- International Atomic Energy Agency (IAEA) – it is to enlarge its ability to review security of nuclear facilities in member states. Already, 900 facilities around the world where fissile materials are stored are monitored. An international non-governmental organization, the Nuclear Threat Initiative (NTI), working with the IAEA, says that there is little hope of keeping nuclear materials out of the wrong hands unless there is a blueprint for a more effective global safeguards system and this would cost something in the region of $30 to $50 million. Work has already started on a new systems design
- International Civil Aviation Organization (ICAO) – it now has a brief to update air safety standards, including perhaps locking cockpits or even arming pilots. A high-level conference called for February 2002 looked at ways of preventing terrorists getting onto aircraft, including possible use of biometric identification techniques (like face-screening and finger printing). Already, controls are in place to ensure tighter checks of luggage and passengers
- International Maritime Organization (IMO) – it is now reviewing key international treaties concerning terrorism on the high seas. A UN Convention entered into force in 1992 to ensure action is taken against those who seize ships by force, commit violence or place explosives there. Ship-owning governments must prosecute and even extradite offenders

- Organization for the Prohibition of Chemical Weapons (OPCW) (new, since 1997) – experts on mobilizing and coordinating international responses to chemical terrorist attacks are devising new and improved strategies and tests, to provide answers to such questions as 'How can chemical weapons be detected?' and 'How can we protect ourselves against chemical attack?' There is to be global tracking of chemicals that can be used to make weapons and challenge inspections to survey stockpiles and production plants
- World Health Organization – they are working all-out to make sure that public health bodies respond quickly to the suspicion of deliberate infections. An informed and responsible public is a critical part of the response. Factsheets on communicable diseases that could be used by bio-terrorists, such as anthrax, bubonic plague or smallpox, are now widely available.

THE UN AND TREATIES AGAINST TERRORISM

The second field of UN counter-terrorism activity is in the field of treaties designed to cast a global net around terrorism. There are twelve major Conventions obliging those states which ratify these measures to do their utmost to flush out terrorists. Most of the United Nations' 185 member states have ratified these Conventions which then come into force after thirty days. This is a list of these treaties with their main provisions:

- Convention on Offences Committed on Board Aircraft (1963) – authorizes the captain to restrain anyone committing or about to commit an act hazarding the aircraft

- Convention for the Suppression of Unlawful Seizure of Aircraft (1970) – makes it an offence for any person on board to seize or exercise control of the aircraft
- Convention for the Suppression of Unlawful Acts against Civil Aviation (1971) (improving the remit of the 1963 act), making it an offence to act violently on the flight or place an explosive
- Convention on the Prevention and Punishment of Attacks on Internationally Protected Persons (1973) – concerned to prevent assaults and assassination attempts on heads of state, ministers, and others entitled to special protection
- International Convention against the Taking of Hostages (1979) – criminalizes the seizure, detention, and threat to kill, of a person in order to bring pressure on a third party (e.g. ransom)
- Convention on the Physical Protection of Nuclear Material (1980) – criminalizes the unlawful possession, transfer, theft and injurious use of nuclear substances
- Protocol for the Suppression of Unlawful Acts at Airports (1988) – takes the 1971 act further to deal with terrorism at airports
- Convention for the Suppression of Unlawful Acts against Maritime Navigation (1988) – makes it an offence to seize or exercise control over a ship by force or to act so violently that safe navigation is in danger
- Convention on the Marking of Plastic Explosives (1991) (negotiated in the aftermath of the 1988 PanAm 103 bombing), to control, detect and render safe plastic explosives by chemical marking
- International Convention for the Suppression of

Terrorist Bombing (1999) – states are obliged to take precautions against bombing, deter and prevent bombers and to use legal means of prosecution and extradition

- International Convention on the Suppression of Terrorism (2001–02) – states are to condemn as criminal and unjustifiable all acts, methods and practices of terrorism and are to take effective counter-action against them.

THE UN AND THE FINANCING OF TERRORISM

Third, there is the major operation to defeat the financing of terrorism. Recognizing that financing of some sort is at the heart of terrorist activity, an all-nations programme headed by the United Nations paves the way for close cooperation and concerted action between financial authorities and law enforcement bodies. Now clamps will be put on sponsors of terrorism and not only on its perpetrators. The US Secretary of Defense, Donald Rumsfeld, has said that the uniforms in this operation will be bankers' pinstripes. All states will be required to adopt their national laws so as to bear down heavily upon rogue banks and shady tax havens. Suspect 'entrepreneurs' will be investigated and a freeze will be put upon their discovered assets. The United Nations, as financial watchdog, will work in harness with President Bush's Foreign Terrorist Asset Tracking Center. At the UN the General Assembly has put on the table an International Covenant for the Suppression of the Financing of Terrorism. Nevertheless, despite all this

NOW CLAMPS WILL BE PUT ON SPONSORS OF TERRORISM AND NOT ONLY ON ITS PERPETRATORS.

counter-terrorism detective work, the task of winkling out terrorism funding is enormously difficult with a number of very small needles to be found in a large number of haystacks. Imagine the problems that dubious financing presents:

- there are hundreds of thousands of money transactions on paper needing scrutiny
- there are just as many 'deals', particularly in the developing world, which are never recorded on paper and which ignore any statutory or border controls. In the 'hawala' system in the Middle East and South-East Asia, huge amounts of cash are passed between brokers 'on a nod, a wink and a promise'. Teasing out the legitimate from the unsavoury looks to be impossible
- some countries such as Iran, Sudan and Pakistan have so-called relief and charitable organizations that are very likely fronts for terrorist activity
- money laundering and drug trafficking divert large amounts of capital into suspect coffers in at least 19 countries according to FBI and MI5 reports. So far, only about $24 million from these sources has been frozen
- the al-Qaida network has very great riches. Its acknowledged head, Osama bin Laden, has scattered millions of dollars across financial and commercial agencies in Europe and the Arab world. Many of his business 'partners' are probably unaware of any connection with him. In Britain, MI5 believes that some 40 individuals and companies are indirectly, perhaps unknowingly, involved with terrorist funding.

THE UN'S RESOLUTIONS AND DEBATE

Finally, in the case of the UN and counter-terrorism, and apart from its building muscle with treaties and Conventions and Resolutions (all binding on members), there has been a remarkable and very public orchestration of sense of outrage and determination to get rid of terrorism (in very general terms). The Security Council quickly framed two Resolutions (1368 and 1373), compelling all the 185 states supporting it to work together against the aiding, supporting, harbouring, organizing and sponsoring of terrorism.

Resolution 1373 of 28 September distinguished between terrorist and non-terrorist crime where the former was intended to intimidate people or to compel a government to certain actions. An Ad-Hoc Committee was set up, chaired by the British Ambassador to the UN, Jeremy Greenstock, to work out speedily the fine detail of the International Convention on Suppression of Terrorism (the last Convention listed above). All states would have to hunt down suspected terrorists, to deny them safe havens, to arrest them, to intensify and accelerate the exchange of information on terrorist actions, movements, and use of communication technologies and falsified documents. The domestic laws of countries touching upon terrorism should be modified to prevent terrorists slipping from one place to another. States must report their actions within ninety days. Earlier Resolutions of the Security Council had demanded that Afghanistan's

THE DOMESTIC LAWS OF COUNTRIES TOUCHING UPON TERRORISM SHOULD BE MODIFIED TO PREVENT TERRORISTS SLIPPING FROM ONE PLACE TO ANOTHER.

Taliban regime act swiftly to close down terrorist training camps and yet another required Taliban to hand over Osama bin Laden to appropriate authorities so that he could face trial.

In the General Assembly, the first week of October 2001 brought representatives of 160 countries together. It was an unprecedented gesture to invite Rudolf Giuliani, Mayor of New York and a dramatic figure standing tall at 'Ground Zero' and '9/11', to open proceedings. For five days the General Assembly held an intensive debate on international terrorism with the goal of amassing a legal arsenal of international treaties to combat the menace in its many forms. A great variety of opinion was raised during those five days but two points raised are especially interesting. There was width in the Assembly's view, 'aware that the new century would bring far-reaching transformations during which forces of aggressive nationalism and religious and ethnic extremism would continue to challenge the international community'. The General Assembly strongly condemned a violation of the right to live free from fear and the right to life, liberty and security. There were also differences of viewpoint. Was it not possible to frame a definition of terrorism? A number of Third World states voiced doubts about the meaning of terrorism as developed countries used it. A more comprehensive understanding of terrorism was necessary which did not refer to situations involving colonialism and its flagrant violations of human rights. Nor did

THE GENERAL ASSEMBLY STRONGLY CONDEMNED A VIOLATION OF THE RIGHT TO LIVE FREE FROM FEAR AND THE RIGHT TO LIFE, LIBERTY AND SECURITY.

the conventional definition take account of alien occupations by racist regimes that might give rise to 'terrorism', so-termed, which was really a legitimate struggle of peoples for self-determination.

Delegates from Lebanon and Syria applauded the heroic resistance of Palestinians against the Israeli occupation of their lands. Israel's domination was 'state terrorism', Cuba, Iraq and Libya agreed that this was so. Further, the Ambassador of Yemen said that those who sought asylum, whatever their origin, should never be regarded as terrorists. In a word, despite everybody's zeal to give priority to counterterrorism, it is the agreed meaning of 'terrorism' that still defeats us.

THE EUROPEAN UNION AND COUNTER-TERRORISM

A smaller constellation of states than the UN, the European Union (EU) has at present twenty-five states as members. The Union works in a great number of fields, economic, social and political. Cooperation in foreign and social policies and in justice and home affairs gives human rights pride of place and so countering terrorism is a demanding priority. Several days after the terrorist strike at the United States, the EU straightaway put in hand an arrangement for partnership in what was to be a highly organized fight against terrorism, focusing on those areas where the Union could provide more than any individual member state. A plan of action was to comprise these and other measures for the European states to implement urgently:

POLICE AND JUDICIAL COOPERATION

- joint investigation teams of police and magistrates
- a common list of terrorist organizations
- exchange of information between national police and Europol (i.e. Interpol)
- non-proliferation and export controls of weapons-grade chemical and bacteriological substances
- rigorous check of procedures for obtaining passports and visas and a fight against forged documents
- judicial and security liaison between the EU and the United States.

DIPLOMATIC FRONT

- staunch support for the United States building of a global coalition against terrorism (see later in this chapter) and staunch support for US military operations in Afghanistan. Total support, also, for the Security Council Resolutions on terrorism
- immediate talks on improving and coordinating European security and defence policies
- complete rejection of any equating of terrorism with the Arab and Muslim world
- a crucial need to kickstart a Middle East peace process (limiting terrorist activities)
- redoubling of sustained EU relief and reconstruction efforts in Afghanistan
- talks with Iran, Pakistan and Palestinian Authority about political, economic and social measures to reduce resort to terrorism

- concrete commitments to fight terrorism to be agreed with non-EU states (e.g. Russia, Norway, Switzerland, other eastern European states, and Israel)
- immediate freeze on detected terrorist assets and programme to investigate others.

HUMANITARIAN AID

- wide-ranging aid to Afghanistan and Iraq to offset terrorism-related destruction, supply of immediate life-saving needs (water, food, shelter, refugee assistance), medico-nutritional projects, infrastructural rebuilding.

AIR TRANSPORT

- measures to improve security at airports and aboard aircraft. Training schemes for aircrew and airport personnel
- consultations about hijacking and other incident prevention.

ECONOMIC AND FINANCIAL MEASURES

- money laundering laws to be tightened
- enquiry into market manipulation and speculation by suspect terrorism supporters
- report on effect of terrorist attacks on tourist areas and companies
- report on effect of terrorist attacks on insurance companies' resources and premiums
- money transfers into and out of Europe will be scrutinized by European banks.

EMERGENCY PREPAREDNESS AGAINST BIOTERRORIST THREATS

- drawing together medical and scientific expertise in information exchange
- inventory of possible biological weapons agents and their treatment
- reinforcing warning systems, surveillance and response capacities
- developing clear, authoritative communication with the public
- planning of stockpiles of antidotes and equipment
- liaison with the World Health Organisation and non-governmental bodies.

A thorough study of Europe's counter-terrorism legislation is beyond the scope of this small book. One or two major points are possible. It is interesting to see in the Council of Europe Convention on the Suppression of Terrorism (1997) and again in the Council of Europe Convention on Terrorism (2005) that each regards extradition as the most effective way of dealing with the individual terrorist. Both Conventions, moreover, emphasize that what they understand to be a 'political offence' must never be a justification for extraditing a suspect. Further, they both state that public provocation, incitement to violence, recruitment, training and ancillary activities are not to be considered political offences. This is supposed to prevent states refusing extradition requests because they consider an accuser's conduct deserves protection as a political act. Almost certainly this view would not be endorsed widely in London or Washington or Madrid. Are not most terrorist groups, contemporary or recent, motivated by political considerations?

Box 5

A terrorist incident

Place

Kutu, island of Bali, Indonesia, 2 October 2002

Incident

- Small bomb in backpack wrecks a crowded bar. A second massive car bomb destroys a nightclub. A third bomb explodes outside the US Embassy.
- 202 are killed, 209 injured. The majority are foreign tourists, especially Australians.

Consequences

- Australia's '9/11' causes great distress there.
- Indonesia's government sees attack as treason by Islamic irredentists. Severe curbs on assembly and movement result.
- Elsewhere, in Australia and USA, concern that attackers were linked to al-Qaida and anti-American targeting. Was there a web of supporters?
- Tourism gravely affected at first but recovers after two years.
- Lengthy and involved legal proceedings charge several Indonesians. Six sentenced subject to appeal. Continuing doubt as to actual motivation.

Another point, perhaps an encouraging circumstance, is that the Commissioner for Human Rights of the Council of Europe has raised concerns about invasions of privacy and freedom of expression and association in the most recent Convention. In the body of the Convention there seems to be a lack of respect for human rights. The notion that there can be a balance between essential human rights and security issues seems to him to represent a fallacy. The protection of human rights is a precondition for any anti-terrorist measure.

THE UNITED STATES AND COUNTER-TERRORISM

A description of the United States gearing up for counter-terrorism is discussed here in three stages, namely, the immediate aftermath in September 2001, then the shaping of a counter-terrorism approach, and finally a look at future policies.

The awesome collapse of the World Trade Center brought home to thoughtful observers a number of excruciating consequences. For the first time, a major world state, and one insulated from the carnage of the First and Second World Wars, had suffered a direct blow of great magnitude at its vibrant heart. Second, the United States had to face the uncomfortable fact of extreme vulnerability. Its defences, always proudly manned, had been breached not by remote-controlled missiles but by nineteen suicidal young men armed only with penknives ('boxcutters'). No costly shield in space like Son of Star Wars would guarantee a

THE UNITED STATES HAD TO FACE THE UNCOMFORTABLE FACT OF EXTREME VULNERABILITY.

nation's security when, as the US Secretary-General put it, 'suicide terrorists know no limit to their audacity, their imagination, and their inhumanity'. Third, in Manhattan's mountain of debris and dust, seven storeys high, there were entombed almost 3,000 victims of eighty different nationalities.

Anger, grief, disbelief, shock – these were the first feelings visible in New York and magnified around the world. In the days that followed, the *Washington Post* and the *New York Times* found space to pose questions. Why are we hated so? What must we do to lower the sense of grievance and injustice out there that leads men to do what they have done here? More immediately, it was the anger that prevailed. And a clamour for action.

President Bush spoke on television of his 'unyielding anger'. What had been launched at the United States was 'evil' in intention and in consequence. Few of his listeners would be ready to search for clarification of 'unyielding' and to spend time working out how, relying on a ground force, anything 'evil' might be fought. Speculations of this kind were to come later. More obvious was the all-round agreement that the allies of the wrongdoers must be found and punished. The operation to do this was to be termed Infinite Justice. (Again, it was not until later that the meaning of 'infinite' and, indeed, of finite justice was to be asked about.)

Counter-terrorism of the sort encountered in other places has generally 'sussed out' a suspect individual or group. Counter-terrorism, like terrorism, benefits from having a target in the sights. For a week or two, in later September, the United States Administration shifted its focus. Was not the evil nature and doing of Osama bin Laden and his leadership of the al-Qaida network the prime consideration? He was wanted – 'dead or alive'. If the Taliban regime in Afghanistan harboured terrorist training camps and gave al-Qaida sanctuary then were we not justified in a military counter-action and that as soon as possible? Given the malevolence of Saddam Hussein in Iraq and the quite likely link between his well-armed regime and Arab terrorists was there not a case for military engagement there, when practicable? And since terrorist cells were now spread globally, then surely counter-terrorism must operate as some sort of universal response?

The shifts in focus were apparent in changing policy options. One senator was heard to remark, perhaps half-seriously, 'Our options are the only options: the others stink!' Apart from this, an evident American need was for friends. An isolated response would be inadequate. Uncle Sam traditionally had stood tall more or less alone to defend United States core interests, save that this time an all-nations counter-action would be more effective, although some members of the Senate were never going to accept that. President Bush, addressing Congress, called for a world coalition to go into battle. He omitted mention of that experienced coalition, the United Nations, which (as we have seen) had been working so hard and so long to combat terrorism. We Are In This Together, he called, as United States diplomats flew everywhere to talk, to cajole, to induce and to bribe governments to come on board. There was a ready agreement to join from most countries and, to Washington's delight, even from the 'somewhat dubious ones', namely, Sudan, Oman, Saudi Arabia, Iran, Syria, Egypt and Indonesia. Hope was springing universally if not eternally. A candid observer might have wondered whether states such as these, so recently tarnished by terrorist activity, would ever stand 'shoulder to shoulder' with a frequently despised United States.

The coalition turned out to be stronger on rhetoric than on physical mobilization. Not only British opinion disliked the idea of giving the Americans a 'blank cheque' with the expected payment of a part in a military adventure. It so happened that Washington decided, for the present and for military reasons, to limit military response to an assault on the terrorist nest in Afghanistan. The hawks had given way to the doves. There was another shift in policy, conforming to strategic decisions. Operation Infinite Justice was to be replaced by Operation Enduring Freedom. In a more positive way, the retaliatory fling of justice as a battlefield idea was moving into a more positive one of helping to reconstitute the shattered, tyrannical and offending land of Afghanistan.

OPERATION INFINITE JUSTICE WAS TO BE REPLACED BY OPERATION ENDURING FREEDOM.

Military operations against Afghanistan began in October 2001 with the mobilization of air and sea forces in the Indian Ocean and in the Persian Gulf. Forty targets in Afghanistan were pinpointed for attack by heavy B52 bombers of the United States Air Force although this much-battered country was described as 'not target-rich'. The rather fragmentary air defence installations, the training camps and bases of al-Qaida, as intelligence satellites had reported them, all these were to be hammered as a preliminary to the despatch, it was hoped, of a multi-national ground force. The resulting engagement ended much more quickly than anyone had fore-cast with the crumbling away of Afghan resistance and the collapse of the Taliban regime. In military terms, however, the United States had done what it had without any help from the coalition apart from a small British special force. Again, in military terms, the United States has worked hard to justify its intervention in Iraq, to remove the arch-terror-ist Saddam Hussein, and, as occupier, to establish stable democracy. Almost predictably, the war in Iraq fails to con-tain inevitable terrorism in a country that is far from pacific.

Inevitably, the nature of this heavy counter-terrorism brings with it heated discussion. The declarations of President Bush that this was 'war', and that the following year, 2002, would be one of continued 'war', have led to much unhappiness. The American President as Commander-in-Chief must strike an inspiring stance as leader but the new vocabulary he used, with its Churchillian tones of 'we will not tire, nor falter, nor fail', irritated many. Apart from the sorties against Afghanistan, how could it be a war against terrorism in gen-eral with no state identified as enemy, no troops out in the open field, no array of weapons, no ceasefire, no point at which defeat or victory could be established? We were used to

THE NEW VOCABULARY HE USED, WITH ITS CHURCHILLIAN TONES OF 'WE WILL NOT TIRE, NOR FALTER, NOR FAIL', IRRITATED MANY.

the idea of a war against a generalized malaise such as poverty, hunger, disease, cancer, crime, but is an overall military response aimed at separate incidents in many countries ever practicable? It does not seem an appropriate means of counter-terrorism. It is, says the editor of the *Guardian*, rather like taking a sledgehammer to crack a flu virus. The Muslim world, in general, thinks that they can never approve of an onslaught which results in so much 'collateral damage' for Muslim civilians. In the early stages of the military response there were those who saw the war as the ultimate form of counter-terrorism, like the American Vice-President, Dick Cheney, who saw it as 'a war that may never end – at least not in our lifetime'.

To be fair to the US Administration and its response to terrorism, not all the counter-action was to rely upon the heavy boots of the US Marine Corps. The Department of Defense, uncertain perhaps about a full-scale mobilization of troops, consulted with the CIA as to the practicability of sending secret agents into troubled terrorist locations although their methods might trouble the liberals. A senior CIA officer in a BBC interview put the matter candidly when asked if results were more important than human rights. 'Yes, within limits ... our work is deep, down and dirty', he replied. The 'liberals' were also worried by proposals from the White House that arrested tourists be put before a military tribunal, not a civil court. For most lawyers this was certainly neither infinite nor finite justice. Would it not mean a parallel justice system with arbitrary detention and no jury? There could be alternatives like the special court set up in the Netherlands for the Lockerbie accused and the War Crimes court, also in the

NO SCHEME FOR DETECTING AND INDICTING TERRORISTS WOULD BE REPUTABLE AND FAIR IF IT DEPENDED UPON A CATCH-ALL CONSPIRACY LAW. Netherlands, at which Slobodan Milosevic and others were being tried. Moreover, no scheme for detecting and indicting terrorists would be reputable and fair if it depended upon a catch-all conspiracy law. Overall, the United States continues to find the thinking out of workable and legitimate counter-terrorism a most taxing business.

FEELING SAFE

The effectiveness of counter-terrorist policies, wherever they are devised, will surely be measured in the light of simple questions whether asked by the bureaucrat or the ordinary family. Where we have got to grips with terrorism are people there beginning to feel safe again in their homes, workplaces and daily lives? Are there fewer suicide attacks on innocent people? Has an end been seen to the hijacking of aircraft? Is the possibility of bioterrorism now less credible? How far can one begin to understand what leads through fear, despair and hatred to violence against others? And, to use a medical analogy, should we first find the root causes of the disease, see how it develops, before we attempt to treat it and curb it? More positively, should not a lot more be done through no-strings aid to help some people live and settle their differences without reaching for weapons?

Ex-President Bill Clinton has said recently of counter-terrorism that an important priority would be to dismantle the 'boxes' in which most of us live, to break down barriers, and to mix more freely and tolerantly with others. Terrorism, he believes, is often the last desperate pitch of the humiliated and the hungry. It is the raw message of those who are neither heard nor understood. Effective counter-terrorism programmes benefit from recruiting not only doers but listeners. In any case, something that President George Bush said as he toured the still-smoking ruins in New York makes sense:

TERRORISM, HE BELIEVES, IS OFTEN THE LAST DESPERATE PITCH OF THE HUMILIATED AND THE HUNGRY.

> Terrorism will be defeated if we are not terrorized. Fear must not rule our lives. They are weak and we are strong – and we will grow stronger.

WHERE TO FIND
OUT MORE

A recent book of mine, Whittaker, David J., *The Terrorism Reader*, published in 2001 by Routledge, features on pages 289–92 a guide to further reading about terrorism as well as comprehensive references on pages 279–88 to twelve case studies. An extensive and up-to-date bibliography is in Laqueur, Walter (1999), *The New Terrorism*, Oxford University Press; Laqueur (2004) *No End to War*.

A point made in the above guide to reading is repeated here. Most people will be able to search for relevant literature and, to some extent, select it, using computer terminals and internet facilities in today's libraries and through the on-line catalogue Amazon (*www.amazon.co.uk*).

Two useful addresses are:
United Nations Information Centre,
Millbank Tower (21st floor),
21–24 Millbank, London SW1P 4QH
United Nations Department of Public Information, Public Enquiries Unit, UN Plaza, New York NY 10017, United States.

These websites will yield a great deal of information:
United Nations
  www.un.org
Terrorism Research Council (USA)
  www.terrorism.com
International Policy Institute for Counter-Terrorism (Herzliya, Israel)
  www.ict.org.il
British Library (UK) Opac 97 Service
  http//opac97.bl.uk

It is always worthwhile putting keywords to a reliable search engine, e.g. terrorism, Oklahoma City, IRA, ETA, Che Guevara, World Trade Center, etc., etc.

A book by an independent intelligence analyst raises disturbing questions about the 2005 London bombing and the mindset of government and security agencies:
Black, Crispin (2005), *7–7 The London Bombs. What went wrong?* London, Gibson Square Books.

A most useful and recent reference work is well-ordered:
Thackrah, John Richard (2004), *Dictionary of Terrorism*, London, Routledge, 2nd edition.

INDEX TO *TERRORISM*